When I heard that my friend Hallie and he.. ..
I was speechless. What could I possibly say or do to help? I was deeply saddened by the news but had absolutely no idea what to say. So I said nothing. I had no words for my friend of over twenty years. Hallie and Shadrach have taken their pain and given us a gift. This beautiful book will help all of us understand these losses in a real and profoundly personal way. I hope you don't need this book, but if you do, you will appreciate the personal and pastoral way Hallie guides you through the thoughts, fears, and tears associated with the road to healing.

PAUL H. ALEXANDER, president,
Hope International University

With authentic expression and vulnerability, Hallie allows her own experiences of loss to tell a story about God's redeeming love and the restoration of a broken heart. The journey of healing is remarkably articulated to provide an understanding of the time, space, support, and comfort needed to normalize the grief process unique to baby loss. Like Abby, this book is a gift from God to minister to the many families who have been left distraught and confused by the loss of children in their lives and offers a hope beyond all understanding.

MELISSA L. ZWART, MS, MA, LMFT,
program director, Azusa Pacific University

This is the book I wish I had after my baby died. Hallie chronicles her own experience in a way that is refreshingly honest, relatable, and practical, and she does not shy away from questioning God in the midst of the deepest pain. Reading *Hope Beyond an Empty Cradle* after experiencing infant loss is like holding the hand of an empathic friend who has traveled the same road—and turns back to offer hope for your journey too.

RACHEL LOHMAN, founder, Hope Again Collective

Hope Beyond an Empty Cradle gives an authentic voice to what has been a mostly silent grief. Through her own story of heartbreak, Hallie Scott has provided a tender validation for those experiencing this often lonely journey. Her subsequent work with other baby loss moms and dads has given her a wealth of practical advice for family and friends who want to support them. For Christian readers she leaves room to question and be angry with God while remembering that he will never leave us nor forsake us. Finally, it is an important book for therapists who work with traumatic grief and PTSD.

Theresa Cornelius, LMFT

HOPE
BEYOND
an
EMPTY
Cradle

HOPE
BEYOND
an
EMPTY
Cradle

THE JOURNEY TOWARD
HEALING AFTER STILLBIRTH,
MISCARRIAGE, AND CHILD LOSS

HALLIE SCOTT

ZONDERVAN
REFLECTIVE

ZONDERVAN REFLECTIVE

Hope Beyond an Empty Cradle
Copyright © 2021 by Hallie Scott

Requests for information should be addressed to:
Zondervan, *3900 Sparks Dr. SE, Grand Rapids, Michigan 49546*

Zondervan titles may be purchased in bulk for educational, business, fundraising, or sales promotional use. For information, please email SpecialMarkets@Zondervan.com.

ISBN 978-0-310-53416-7 (audio)

Library of Congress Cataloging-in-Publication Data

Names: Scott, Hallie, author.
Title: Hope beyond an empty cradle : the journey toward healing after stillbirth, miscarriage, and child loss / Hallie Scott.
Description: Grand Rapids : Zondervan, 2021.
Identifiers: LCCN 2021003609 (print) | LCCN 2021003610 (ebook) | ISBN 9780310534143 (paperback) | ISBN 9780310534150 (ebook)
Subjects: LCSH: Miscarriage. | Children—Death. | Miscarriage—Psychological aspects. | Miscarriage—Religious aspects—Christianity.
Classification: LCC RG648 .S263 2021 (print) | LCC RG648 (ebook) | DDC 618.3/9—dc23
LC record available at https://lccn.loc.gov/2021003609
LC ebook record available at https://lccn.loc.gov/2021003610

All Scripture quotations, unless otherwise indicated, are taken from the ESV® Bible (The Holy Bible, English Standard Version®). Copyright © 2001 by Crossway, a publishing ministry of Good News Publishers. Used by permission. All rights reserved.

Scripture quotations marked NIV are taken from The Holy Bible, New International Version®, NIV®. Copyright © 1973, 1978, 1984, 2011 by Biblica, Inc.® Used by permission of Zondervan. All rights reserved worldwide. www.Zondervan.com. The "NIV" and "New International Version" are trademarks registered in the United States Patent and Trademark Office by Biblica, Inc.®

Any internet addresses (websites, blogs, etc.) and telephone numbers in this book are offered as a resource. They are not intended in any way to be or imply an endorsement by Zondervan, nor does Zondervan vouch for the content of these sites and numbers for the life of this book.

All rights reserved. No part of this publication may be reproduced, stored in a retrieval system, or transmitted in any form or by any means—electronic, mechanical, photocopy, recording, or any other—except for brief quotations in printed reviews, without the prior permission of the publisher.

Cover Design: Studio Gearbox
Cover Images: © Iamkaoo99/Shutterstock; © damerau/Shutterstock
Interior Design: Denise Froehlich

Printed in the United States of America

21 22 23 24 25 /LSC/ 10 9 8 7 6 5 4 3 2 1

For Abby

CONTENTS

ABBY

Delight yourself in the LORD,
and he will give you the desires of your
heart.

—PSALM 37:4

It was 4:30 a.m. on a Sunday in early August.

When I awoke, I was already hot. I expected that. My body felt like an incubator, given that I was thirty-nine weeks pregnant. Throughout my pregnancy, women had told me that summers were the worst time to be pregnant and that I would be hot. They weren't wrong. I was hot multiplied by one thousand.

I was awakened by what I thought were labor pains. I had nothing to compare these pains to because this was my first pregnancy. The pain was enough to wake me but not so painful that I thought something was wrong. My thoughts immediately went to my C-section. My baby was in a breech position and had been the entire pregnancy. I didn't like the options available to try to turn the baby manually, so I had scheduled a cesarean delivery. Yet I still had nine days to go before that appointment. Why was I having contractions? The nurse hadn't covered this scenario in my birthing class. I had expected to go into surgery and deliver a baby without going into labor or experiencing labor pains.

My husband, Shadrach, and I had to get up in less than two hours to go to church, and I was a first-time mom, so I decided to rely on what I had heard in the birthing class: relax and wait. Although I was conflicted about this, I chose to hold on to what I had learned. But I did not sleep. I lay awake in bed, questioning myself. *Do I wait, or do I need to do something?* The pain wasn't terrible, and my husband was sound asleep. *Do I wake him? Do we need to call the doctor?*

I had also just seen the doctor less than forty-eight hours before, and at that appointment everything had been great. My baby, who we had learned at twenty weeks was a girl, seemed healthy. I had been able to see my baby girl "practicing" her breathing, I had heard the heartbeat, and she had looked perfect. I hadn't started to dilate and had no reason to believe anything was wrong. So why was I now having labor pains?

As soon as my husband woke up, sometime before seven o'clock that morning, we called the doctor. She was very kind on the phone. She normalized my anxiety and told us to go to the hospital to get checked. She didn't sound concerned, nor did she say she was worried.

AT THE HOSPITAL

We arrived at the hospital at about quarter after seven, and I was taken back to a room to check my baby's heartbeat. I felt a little anxious. I didn't want to overreact to what was probably normal, and I didn't believe I would have a baby that day. I had carried my baby for nine months, and the plan was that she would join us in another nine days. She wasn't supposed to come yet; that wasn't the plan.

Shadrach and I had just finished setting up the nursery the day before. We hadn't put the car seat in the car, I hadn't packed my hospital bag, and I hadn't even brought the diaper bag with us to the hospital. In my mind, I kept repeating that I still had nine days.

I still planned to write thank-you notes later that day for shower gifts I had received the previous weekend. I expected to go to work the next day. I was supposed to see clients one last time before I went on maternity leave. I believed I still had time to do all the things that needed to get done before we became a family of three.

I fluctuated between feelings of anxiety and excitement that I would soon be able to see my baby girl's face in an ultrasound. Throughout my pregnancy, whenever we went in for an ultrasound, she did the exact opposite of what the technicians needed. If they wanted to see her from one angle, she quickly moved to the opposite perspective. During one of the first ultrasounds I had, she "ran" up my uterus to "avoid" the technician's wand. So I hadn't seen a clear image of her face yet. She was my noncompliant girl. And that morning, it seemed she was still living according to her own rules by possibly joining us before I was ready.

I was excited to meet my baby. I wouldn't have to wonder anymore what she looked like; I would know. I could stop pondering whether she had a lot of hair or who she looked like more, my husband or me. Before long I would be holding my baby girl in my arms. It never occurred to me that something could be wrong.

After the nurse brought me back to a room, she strapped me up to the fetal Doppler and began to search for a heartbeat. In the past, other nurses had trouble finding the heartbeat, so I didn't worry immediately; my girl liked to be difficult. But after a few moments that felt like hours, I became concerned. I tried telling myself my baby was okay. I practiced what I often told others: I tried to stick with the known truth at that moment.

Still, the nurse couldn't find a heartbeat. By this point, my husband had joined me as well. When the nurse brought in an ultrasound machine and another person, that was the moment I became scared.

Everything shifted into a blur. I remember the new person—a technician or a nurse—had trouble turning on the machine, and my anxiety grew. I remember him saying, "How do I turn this thing on?" I was now terrified. He began searching for the heartbeat without saying a word. Years later, I can't picture his face, but I can still see him staring intently at the screen. Isn't it funny what the brain remembers?

After a moment, another gentleman joined us—I assume a doctor. I'm sure he told me his name, but I don't remember it. He spoke the words that broke me: "I'm sorry. There is no heartbeat."

In that second, my brain did something I can't explain. All at once, I went into a dissociative place while simultaneously straining to hear what was happening. It was as if half my brain had shut down and the other half had gone hypervigilant. My mind was trying to make sense of the information given, but it just didn't make sense. How could there be no heartbeat? I tried to stay connected to what was said, but I desperately wanted to run away, back to a time when my baby girl was alive and healthy, with a strong heartbeat.

I don't remember the few moments between hearing those words and my tears starting. I wasn't aware of the doctor's leaving, how I transitioned into an actual hospital room, or how long it took. I do remember being aware of other women around me, although I couldn't see them.

In those moments, my world shattered.

What I didn't know until much later was that the way I experienced the world had changed forever. The world became unsafe. Losing my baby girl altered the way I experience relationships and view the world. It also changed the way I experience God.

Once I was in a regular hospital room, the on-call doctor came in, sat with us, and explained our options. I could have labor induced and wait up to twenty-four hours to deliver my baby naturally, or I could have a C-section immediately. I chose the second option for a couple of reasons. First, I knew that if my baby were alive, a C-section posed less risk, and even though I knew she had died, I needed my baby not to be hurt. As her mother, I still needed to protect my baby from any harm.

Second, I chose the C-section because I had an overwhelming need to hold my daughter. I didn't want to wait a day;

I needed it now. I needed her to be in my arms, and I needed to see her and touch her. I needed to know she was real.

Somewhere between the on-call doctor giving me my options and the surgery, my regular doctor showed up. She was amazing. She sat with us, and I am sure she told me something about the procedure, although I don't remember her words. What I do remember was her tenderness. In the sterile environment of a hospital room, she sat with me on my hospital bed and rubbed my pregnant belly with a tenderness that conveyed that my daughter was loved. My doctor, a woman I had come to trust, had walked with me through my pregnancy. I am grateful she walked with me through delivery.

Because I was in a state of shock, it didn't occur to me that I was going to have surgery. It didn't dawn on me that I would be admitted to the hospital and stay there. When the nurse came in to prep me for my C-section, I was genuinely surprised.

The preparation and wait time for the surgery was about three hours. The day is cataloged in my memory like an unfinished photo album. Some snapshots are clear and permanent, while others are nowhere to be found. I remember being walked into the operating room. It was so cold that I shivered. I was in a fog-like state. The anesthesiologist said something to me, but it didn't connect; I think he repeated it three times before it registered. I thought, *I am about to see my daughter, who is dead; how can you expect me to do anything you ask?* I sat on the operating table, still shivering, and was asked to bend over for an epidural. However, the snapshot of lying down on the table is gone, as is the one of receiving the anesthesia.

I had no idea when my husband joined me in the room or how he got there. I don't remember seeing him or the doctor before the surgery. I don't know how long the C-section took. I know that, out of kindness, I was allowed to be "put under" through the procedure. My understanding is that I did a lot of talking during the surgery. I was told that I asked if the doctor was in the room at least six times during the surgery.

My husband sat by my side during the procedure. He did not get the gift of the moments of not knowing what was happening. Sometimes I still struggle with guilt for leaving him alone in that. He must have had many thoughts and emotions during those moments. He had to witness the doctor delivering our dead child.

The snapshot that will remain with me forever is what I heard when I woke up. My doctor leaned over and whispered into my ear, "She is beautiful."

She was right. My baby girl was beautiful. She was six pounds and nineteen inches long, and she appeared perfect in every way. She had long fingers, big cheeks, and my husband's toes. Abby was born with a curl on top of her head, exactly like I had as a newborn.

Our daughter, Abigail Elizabeth, was delivered at thirty-nine weeks, within hours of our hearing she had no heartbeat.

ABBY

We named her Abigail because, in our discussions of what to name our daughter, we had read that it means "gift from God." Elizabeth is a family name, and we gave her that middle name to honor my mother.

Most days I can hold the truth that Abby was a gift from God. The gift of Abby has allowed me to feel love deeper than I knew possible. But I have also felt more profound pain than I knew existed.

My daughter was gone, and I felt as if I had been shattered. In a millisecond, I went from a woman excited for the future to what felt like a mirror broken into tiny little shards. Even if the pieces could be put back together, one would always be missing. Touching those shards created so much bleeding and pain, I wondered if the healing process was worth it. Could I just stay a shattered, bleeding mess? Did I even want to try to put the pieces back together?

After I returned to my hospital room, the nurses asked if I wanted to see my daughter.

I finally was able to hold my girl. What a surreal moment. She fit perfectly into my arms, so light and so peaceful. But she wasn't breathing. She was utterly beautiful and looked as if she were sleeping. In the moments of meeting my daughter for the first time, I was also saying goodbye.

My nurse was very kind as she took care of Abby and me. She offered me the option of bathing her, but because my legs were still numb from surgery, I was unable to stand. I watched instead as she lovingly bathed our baby girl. Even now, years later, I can still picture the sweet smile the nurse had as she washed Abby. That precious memory will always be with me.

We had Abby in the room with us for the rest of the day. We held her on and off the entire afternoon, and during the afternoon some friends and family came by to meet and say goodbye to Abby. This happened only because my husband is amazing. He was a pillar of strength that day and called friends and family. He was the one who invited people in. He was my rock.

One gift I will forever appreciate are the pictures we took. A photographer from a nonprofit organization came in and photographed our sweet girl. He was a godsend. He was respectful in how he handled and placed our girl and showed such care to our baby.

I know some people don't want pictures of their child after a stillbirth. But those pictures I have are a priceless gift. I don't get to have school pictures or yearly family portraits. They are the only ones I will have of my daughter, and I cherish them.

Abby was taken away in the early evening. We had spent the afternoon memorizing our daughter's features and saying goodbye. When the nurse came to take Abby, I was alone because my husband had gone home to take care of some things and bring back some necessities for us to remain in the hospital. I watched my daughter being wheeled out in her bassinet, knowing she was going to the morgue. The only images I have of morgues come from TV shows—cold, dark, and scary places. I watched as my daughter went to that place without me. I could no longer protect her. I can't even put into words the feelings that went through me.

Cognitively I knew it wasn't my daughter who was going to the morgue; it was her body. I believed she was, and is, safe and happy in heaven. But at that moment, it felt as if I was sending my daughter to a dark and scary place.

My daughter, part of my heart, was taken from me, and I would not see her again this side of heaven. The hospital room became tiny and dark. My shattered world became overwhelmingly lonely, and it wasn't a loneliness that people can fill. It was an emptiness that remains because that space belongs to my daughter.

I was never able to hear my baby girl cry that day or any day since. I have not heard her laugh or speak her first words. I don't get to know what her favorite color is or if she loves chocolate as much as I do. I will never be able to know her.

Life after Abby

My husband and I spent the next three days in the hospital. The first night was especially hard for both of us. We were both exhausted, physically and emotionally, and the nurses continued to do their job. They routinely checked on me throughout the night as they were supposed to. They kept doing life. In all the world around us, life went on.

I, however, was stuck in bed because I was shaking too badly to stand, a side effect of the surgery, coupled with my grief. I was wishing life would stop. I wanted to wake up from this horrible nightmare and hear my baby cry. I wanted to be exhausted because my daughter was keeping me awake. I wanted to be anxiously trying to figure out how to be a new mom.

Instead, we were in the maternity ward of a hospital without our baby. For the next three days, I never left that room. On the other side of that hospital room door, families were celebrating their healthy children. When the door opened, I could hear a newborn baby crying and new parents laughing. I knew that if I went anywhere outside that room, I would come face-to-face with newborn babies and happy people.

How would I have managed that? At that moment, I hated everyone there with their babies. Why did they get to have their babies and I didn't? What had I done wrong that Abby had died?

Slowly, I recovered from a surgery that had left me empty. The physical symptoms were a continual reminder that my baby had died. I struggled with feelings of betrayal—by my body, by life, and by God. And worst of all, I struggled with the belief that I had failed my daughter, that I was the reason she had died.

Without knowing it, I began to search for the reason this had happened. We have all heard the phrase "Things happen for a reason." If this is true, then the only thing that made sense was that I had done something to cause my daughter's death. I had somehow failed my daughter. Or I had done something wrong against God and he was punishing me. In either option, I was the reason Abby had died.

The alternative was even more horrible. If I was mistaken and wasn't the cause, then how could God do this to me? How could he allow me to carry my sweet Abby for nine months only to take her away from me? How could he dangle my desire for a child in front of me like a carrot? My view of a kind and caring God broke.

After three days, I was wheeled out of the hospital, knowing that I was leaving my daughter in the morgue. I had vowed to protect her. I had carried her for thirty-nine weeks, loved her, and dreamed of who she would be, only to leave her in a cold hospital basement.

We returned to the house we had prepared for Abby, but without Abby. It no longer felt like home.

I returned to the life I had left, even though it was supposed to have changed. Life no longer felt safe.

My husband and I chose not to have a memorial service for Abby. We talked about it and agreed that memorials are an excellent way for people to come together and celebrate a person's life. Although Abby was loved and cherished, we didn't believe we had much to celebrate. We chose to have Abby's body cremated.

About a week after we were home from the hospital, we had an appointment to pick up our daughter's ashes at the mortuary. We stopped for coffee on the way, thinking it would help ease the pain or provide a distraction. I felt confident during the ride. I thought I was prepared to go. How could I hurt any more than I already did?

When we arrived at the mortuary, we were put in a conference room and waited for about five minutes before a woman joined us. As soon as she walked into the room with a bag in her hands, which I knew contained Abby's remains, I began to cry.

She handed us the tiny cap that Abby had worn in the hospital, along with the stuffed bear that held the tiny urn with Abby's ashes, and I was immediately brought back to the reality that Abby was not with us, that she had died. I was holding the ashes of my daughter.

Our "Abby bear" still has a special place in our home.

About a month after we picked up the ashes, my husband and I had a private memorial for our daughter. We found a peaceful spot to place her ashes and said our goodbyes. That spot remains a reverent place for me. I find solace there, and I believe Abby would have liked it.

CARRYING THE GRIEF

In the beginning of my grief journey, I tried to make sense of why Abby died. I struggled with why God allowed this to happen and what I was supposed to do with it. I had been a therapist for about ten years and had been trained to help people through grief. The traditional model suggests that to heal from grief, we need to move through it. But when my baby died, this traditional thinking didn't fit. As I worked through my loss, I realized I didn't want to let go of the grief. Within the grief is where I held the memory of my daughter.

According to common understanding, holding on to grief meant I would stay stuck and not heal. But as I found ways to carry my grief, I grew stronger. My story became one of healing with grief rather than healing and letting go of grief.

A few years after Abby died, I felt called to begin serving baby-loss moms in my work as a therapist. I didn't want others to have the same experience I had when I sought counseling, and that I've heard from many others. I've had the privilege of meeting some amazing women who have taught me a lot and gave me the honor of knowing their babies.

We need a new way to look at grief. We need to recognize that grief is not something we need to let go of or pathologize. I would like to suggest that people do not get stuck in grief. My prayer is that this book will help you realize that. I pray it allows those touched by baby-loss to find hope.

Questions for Reflection

Why did you decide to read this book?

What do you hope to find in the upcoming chapters? What do you want to take away from them?

Does anything from Abby's story remind you of your own experience with child loss or that of a friend?

If you have experienced child loss, how was your experience different from this story?

Chapter 2

MISCARRIAGE

In my work with baby-loss moms, I've heard many tragic stories. One of these came from a woman who learned she was pregnant after weathering a health scare with her husband. She was very excited and secretly hoped for a girl.

Within the first month, she learned that the pregnancy wasn't viable. Her doctor labeled it a chemical pregnancy. A chemical pregnancy is an early pregnancy loss. It happens before an ultrasound sees the fetus but after a positive pregnancy test. In layman's terms, she would suffer a miscarriage.

At that moment, her heart broke. Her dreams of her daughter ended, and she, like many, wondered if she may have caused this.

The actual passing of fetal tissue happened when she wasn't home. She had agreed to go to a family gathering, and because the pregnancy hadn't been announced yet, she kept her obligation. During this family party, she excused herself to the restroom and began to pass clots. When she saw the remnants of the fetal tissue, like many women, she held them as she would a full-term baby.

Then, because there was nothing else to do, she said goodbye and disposed of the fetal tissue.

She returned to the family gathering, stifling her tears and shoving her feelings deep inside. She was among family members, most of whom didn't know she was pregnant, so she acted as if everything were normal. But on the inside, she worked hard to minimize her loss and talk herself out of her sadness. She grieved alone.

MISCARRIAGE

This woman's story shares many similarities with those of others who have miscarried. Many pass the fetal tissue away from home, often in public venues. Imagine attending a professional football game with unknowing friends, only to suffer a miscarriage in the restroom. You then return to the game, acting as if all is well, cheering on your team.

If the loss of the baby is farther along, but before the twenty-week mark, women may be given the option of enduring a dilation and curettage (D&C) after learning their pregnancy is not viable. A D&C is a surgical procedure that involves dilation of the cervix and the removal of the uterine lining. Many women find that their first reaction to an unviable pregnancy is denial. It is common for women who have been scheduled for a D&C to ask for an additional ultrasound "just to be sure" there is no heartbeat. Depending on the relationship with the doctor, this may or may not happen.

The word *miscarriage* brings different thoughts and

emotions to each person. Some take little notice when they hear the word because they have no experience with it. Others hear *miscarriage*, connect it to someone they know, and then move on; it's sad but doesn't affect them directly. Some might even judge a woman for the way she handles her loss: "She should be over it by now." But for many, the word can bring back a flood of emotions, reminding them of their own loss. Miscarriage can create a wound that reopens whenever the topic is mentioned. It is important to allow room for these emotions. They are valid and do not need to be dismissed.

According to the Mayo Clinic the technical definition of miscarriage is a spontaneous loss of a pregnancy before the twentieth week.[1] (Stillbirth, then, is a loss at twenty weeks or after, which occurs in about twenty-four thousand pregnancies a year in the US .)[2] But really, miscarriage is the loss of your baby; it could be your first loss or your seventh. According to the American Pregnancy Association, miscarriage happens in roughly 10 to 25 percent of known pregnancies in the US. Most women are touched in some way by miscarriage, either through their own loss or through someone they know.

The American Pregnancy Association reveals that the most common cause of miscarriage during the first twelve weeks is a chromosomal abnormality.[3] This is usually the result of a damaged egg or sperm. Other causes of miscarriage include infection, health issues in the mom, such as a chronic disease or autoimmune disorder, and abnormalities in the uterus or implantation.

Miscarriage is *not* something you caused. In our journey to make sense of the senseless, we often hear and tend to believe the rationales. We look for answers by googling causes of miscarriages, and we read stories on the internet. We conclude that we must have done something wrong. But there is no scientific backing to suggest that you worked out too hard, ran too fast, or ate something that caused a miscarriage. The miscarriage did not occur because God is punishing you. Even if you weren't thrilled when you discovered the positive pregnancy test, you still did not cause this.

Scientific research does suggest that if you are using illegal drugs or have a history of illegal drug usage, miscarriage is more likely. Drinking and smoking while pregnant also increase your risk for miscarriage. If this is your story and you have suffered from an unintentional miscarriage, please allow yourself grace. It seems plausible that your intent with these behaviors was not to harm your child. Allow yourself grace in your intention. If you find yourself in this scenario, you might be tempted to engage in further behavior to help mask the feelings you are carrying. This could be a good time to find outside help, a professional to talk with to find a new path of healing.

If you are currently experiencing or have experienced a loss through miscarriage, you know it can be overwhelming. The experience and resulting emotions deserve to be honored. You may experience a flood of emotions or quickly flip from one feeling to the next, moving from sad to blazing angry within seconds. This is normal. You are not overreacting, nor are you being dramatic. Please allow yourself time to heal.

Sometimes we gauge our experience and how we should feel based on others' opinions, those who have had a similar experience or people who share life with us. As a result, we often, in essence, lie to ourselves. If we base our feelings on someone else's experience, we may miss how we are actually doing. This experience is yours and yours alone.

Some believe that because the loss was early in the pregnancy, there is no reason to be sad. We tell ourselves it wasn't *really* a baby, so we shouldn't feel grief. It was a blip, and "I can get pregnant again." Why would we cry over something that wasn't really anything yet anyway? This minimizes our feelings and experience. The truth is this: There was a pregnancy, and there was hope for a child. That hope was taken away. There is a reason to be sad.

Or maybe you didn't even want to get pregnant at that moment, so you believe you don't have the right to be sad. Or the sadness comes out of nowhere, and you try to reason it away. Have you ever watched the show *Friends*? There's an episode in which Rachel believes she may be pregnant even though she wasn't trying to have a baby. She takes a pregnancy test but can't bring herself to look at it, so she hands it to her friend Phoebe to tell her the result. Phoebe tells her it is negative, and Rachel starts crying. Rachel says, "How can I be upset over something I never had?" This is the same message many women who have miscarried tell themselves. Allowing yourself permission to have whatever feeling comes up is the most healing thing you can do for yourself, regardless of other people's words or actions. The only path to healing is through the pain.

If you've had multiple miscarriages, the pain of each one can pile up, creating layers of loss. Each loss may trigger feelings from the previous ones. If you have unresolved feelings from a previous loss, they will show up again. The most recent loss may feel more significant than the others, causing you to wonder if you have adequately grieved previous losses. You may feel as if you aren't moving forward. Still, this doesn't necessarily mean you aren't grieving or moving forward.

In the layers of these losses, remember that each loss has its own story. Each story deserves a moment, and you are not stuck. Allow yourself time to heal, and honor your stories.

If you were pregnant with twins and you endured the death of one of your children, another layer of emotion can arise. Parenting only one of your twins can bring about years of longing for your child, seeing both your children in your living child, and comparing the living kid with the one you never saw grow up. Please recognize your grief, and place it where it belongs. Allow yourself to be fully with your living child, and carry your lost child with you.

No one has the right to minimize the grief of a miscarriage, nor do they have a right to push someone into ignoring their pain. We can't devalue someone else's experience, regardless of our own.

A misconception is that men don't usually bond to the baby until much further into the pregnancy. While this is true for some, it is unfair to suggest that is it true for all husbands and partners. Men may have strong feelings of loss that are overlooked due to this belief. Although men don't have the privilege of experiencing firsthand the feelings of pregnancy, including the physical changes or the hormonal shift, their grief surrounding the loss needs to be validated. Too many times friends and family reach out to check in on the wife but assume the husband is fine. It is important that both members of the couple be surrounded.

Husbands and partners have their own experience surrounding loss. Sometimes it feels as if they are guilty of minimizing the experience. I hear from many husbands who, in their grief, don't want to talk about it with their partner because their partner is already struggling: "I can't put this on her too." The husband feels compelled to carry his sadness alone. This is coupled with the discomfort of seeing his wife so sad and feeling powerless to fix it. Men often find value in working to make sure their partner is happy and well taken care of. Many men see themselves as "fixers," and in trying to "fix" the situation many wives can feel missed in the emotion, and in turn, the husband's effort is missed as well. Both partners can be left feeling alone and wishing for connection.

This sentiment is common: "It was your first pregnancy. It's fine; you'll get pregnant again. It happened to me too, and look, I have three kids." In an attempt to help normalize the experience, well-intentioned friends or family members may convey the message that there is no reason to be sad and that you just need to move on. Instead of providing true support, this may result in hiding your sadness. But when a woman pushes down emotions they deem unreasonable, the feelings often won't go away, and instead the woman feels both sad and alone.

As a society, can we do better? Can we make room for a new path of healing? When women and men are left believing they are too dramatic and thinking they are sadder than they should be, they are forced to manage this traumatic event by themselves. It seems less frightening to pretend they are fine than to open themselves up to being told they are too dramatic, too emotional, or too sensitive. Yet if they continue to hear the message "move on and get over it," then the conversation surrounding grief—a vital component to the healing process—can't continue.

There is no such thing as being too impacted by a loss.

Honoring Our Pain

One of the challenges of honoring your sadness in a miscarriage is that there is nothing physical to mourn because the loss is often so early there is no physical body to see and hold. So what are you to do? Minimizing your sorrow is not a good option; it isn't fair to you or your baby. The grief will linger until you give it the respect it deserves.

It can be helpful to have a tangible item you can hold on to as a representation of your child: an ultrasound picture, an item that was purchased in the excitement of your pregnancy, or maybe a teddy bear. Some women buy onesies to share the pregnancy news with their husbands. That's a great representation of your child to keep. Other families plant a tree or flower in honor of their baby.

Navigating Relationships

Your grief can become even more complicated if friends around you are pregnant. How do you support a friend or family member when you are working hard not to be envious because they have what you want? How do you continue to watch their belly grow when yours isn't? How do you maintain a friendship when you can't talk about the only thing they want to talk about—being pregnant?

It is essential for the relationship that the people involved make room for both sides of the situation. If you are the one who is pregnant while supporting a woman through miscarriage, that is difficult. It often creates fear or survivor's guilt. These feelings are as reasonable as grief over the miscarriage.

Survivor's guilt occurs when these types of thoughts emerge: *She should be the pregnant one; she wanted it more* or *I didn't even want to be pregnant*. Journeying through a friend's miscarriage while you are pregnant can bring up the fear of your own vulnerability to miscarriage or loss of your child. Women often feel more connected to their own pregnancy as a result of a friend's miscarriage. They want to hold more tightly to what they fear could be lost.

On the other side of that relationship, listening to and supporting a pregnant friend after just suffering a miscarriage is intensely difficult. Feigning excitement when your heart is broken can be exhausting. Allow time to reflect on what you can give in any moment instead of pushing through. Pushing through will often only make you feel depleted after, which often leads to resentment. Sometimes being strong means allowing yourself a moment. This doesn't mean you need to step out of the friendship; it doesn't even mean taking a break. It means you should give yourself permission to be honest.

If you're invited to a baby shower, ask yourself if you have the emotional capacity to attend. Do you need to create a boundary to feel comfortable while there? Does that boundary look like attending only a portion of the baby shower, followed by self-care afterward? This may appear selfish, and some people may not understand your need for boundaries. But a moment of perceived selfishness may be necessary to keep the friendship.

The baby-loss journey becomes even more complicated and painful when we watch our friends celebrate the delivery of healthy babies. We stand by and celebrate with our friends at first birthday parties while our hearts grieve the loss of our own children. We hear the stories of breastfeeding and potty training, wishing to chime in with our own stories. We long for what others have.

Struggling with jealousy is common. We see happy lives with children and wish for that life. We spend time wishing for what others have, often missing out on what we have. Allow yourself time to reflect on the things in your life you do enjoy. Maybe find a new hobby or passion and make time for it. Search for balance.

Strength can be found when we lean into our sadness. Be honest with yourself and with your friends and family, allowing for flexibility. If at this moment it is too much to be with a certain friend, tomorrow will be a new and different day. It may feel personal and unfair that this loss affects your relationships. Allow those thoughts and feelings, and have an honest conversation with your friend. Today does not determine tomorrow.

Remind Yourself of the Truth

While women are healing after a miscarriage, layers of fear often develop. Many women grow up dreaming of being a mother. When a miscarriage happens, we can spiral into the unknown of "what if?"

"What if I can't get pregnant?" "What if I can get pregnant but my body won't sustain a pregnancy?" "What if I did something to cause this?" These fears often increase with multiple miscarriages, and they have caused some women to avoid early and appropriate medical care. They fear hearing bad news, so they stay in fear of the what-ifs. Please don't allow your fear to get in the way of caring for yourself.

Staying in the present is also essential; practice being

mindful. Mindfulness is something that many therapists practice and is often used in the therapeutic process. Simply put, it is the practice of staying in the present, being aware of your surroundings, and becoming aware of what is going on inside you, or maybe what you are avoiding. It takes practice. It takes moments of checking in with yourself throughout the day.

I often encourage people to begin asking themselves out loud, "How am I?" It takes just seconds to check in with yourself, and many people are often surprised at how long they have been just going through the motions without knowing how they feel.

Take a moment to notice things such as these: *Am I having a physical reaction? If I am feeling a physical response, where am I feeling it in my body? Have I felt it before? What are my thoughts being drawn to? Am I afraid?*

We can easily get caught up in the fear and the resulting lies that occur. Our brains will always conjure up lies when we sit in fear. But we can't see the future, and our pregnancy history does not necessarily determine our future pregnancies. Take time to recognize whether your thoughts are valid. Are they based in truth or your perceptions of the moment? Questioning the future might suggest that fear is the driving force behind your thoughts; take time to validate the fear and look for the truth. This is not the same as talking yourself out of your feelings. This is not giving yourself a pep talk. It is reminding yourself of the truth.

You Can't Prepare for Sadness

Three months after Abby died, I discovered I was again pregnant. This pregnancy wasn't planned, and I felt fear mixed with relief, all topped off with sadness. I wasn't at all ready to be pregnant. I grieved and longed for Abby. It was the beginning of the holiday season, and I wondered how I would survive Christmas.

I was relieved that we would have a child on earth. I was happy that Abby would have a sibling.

When I told Shadrach, this was one of the only times I have been able to read emotion on his face. He was terrified. He saw a friend the next day, and she said she could see the terror in his eyes. He wasn't ready to go through another pregnancy.

We learned in December, during my first doctor's appointment, that my pregnancy wasn't viable. I was shocked. When I learned about this new pregnancy, I focused my worry on the delivery, expecting something similar to my previous experience. When I learned the pregnancy wasn't viable, I was not prepared.

Shadrach says this news tore off the scab that had formed on the Abby wound. He was flooded with renewed grief and memories of losing Abby.

We journeyed through the first holidays without Abby, knowing I was going to miscarry. We chose not to tell our family about the pregnancy. I wasn't ready for the comments and conversation.

I was scheduled for a D&C in early January.

Women who have endured a miscarriage often explain that they withhold excitement in new pregnancies. They convince themselves that "it won't work out anyway." You can't prepare your heart for sadness. Trying to protect yourself from a loss by not getting attached is a lie. The truth is that losing a child hurts. You deserve to feel sad.

Another lie born out of fear is that miscarriage defines a woman's value. I've heard women get caught up in the notion that they were supposed to be moms. Their purpose was to raise children, and their value is derived only from that ability. That simply isn't true. Our worth is based on our humanness. You are valuable because you are you, not because of what you offer.

It is common to experience anger from a miscarriage—at the situation, at pregnant people, and at our bodies. Sometimes there is anger at God. *Why did he allow my baby to be taken away?* Feeling angry is perfectly reasonable. God is bigger than our anger, and he can handle it. There is nothing wrong with feeling mad at the loss of something you had been praying for. Too many times I hear people try to pretend they are not angry with God when they are. I hear from others that we are not allowed to be angry with God. But healing comes through being honest and open to whatever feelings arise. Anger will not last forever.

We have the privilege of moving forward and through our emotions, not moving on from our feelings. We don't get over our feelings. When we move through them and allow them to become part of our story, we become more whole. This journey is not an easy one. Leaning into the discomfort of our sadness and fear is never something we want to do. Often we run from it. But the more we can enter into that sacred space, the stronger we will become.

When supporting a friend who has experienced miscarriage, it is important to remember that the experience is hers and hers alone. The experience may mimic another, or feel familiar, but it will have its own intricacies. Friends and family are vital to support healing and can offer so much comfort. But a woman who is grieving a pregnancy needs space, space that is only defined by what she needs. If she can't articulate what she needs, then allow room for those needs to be seen. Friends don't need to take it upon themselves to fill that space. There can be so much healing for her if she is allowed just to be.

The author of Ecclesiastes writes that God has ordained

> a time to kill, and a time to heal;
> a time to break down, and a time to build up;
> a time to weep, and a time to laugh;
> a time to mourn, and a time to dance (3:3–4).

If you've experienced miscarriage, remember that wherever you are in the moment, God will be with you in it.

Questions for Reflection

If you have experienced miscarriage, what was one thing that encouraged you?

Which words do you wish you had heard while you were healing from a miscarriage?

If you are helping a friend heal from a miscarriage, what is this experience like for you? Have any feelings come up for you that you didn't expect?

Chapter 3

NOW WHAT?

Chances are good that you are reading this book because you or someone you love has either just suffered a miscarriage or said goodbye to their child. You are searching for answers and looking for ways to feel better. I am so sorry you're in this place; I wish you had received the happy ending you were praying for. I also wish I could tell you there's a quick fix or magic words to take the pain away. But these things don't exist.

What I can tell you is that even though you will have moments that feel as if the pain will never end, you can bear this burden. You will grow stronger to carry the weight of the pain, and you can manage it. It will not crush you. In the moments when the pain feels never-ending, remind yourself of your strength. If you think you aren't strong enough, this is a lie. You *can* carry this. If you are struggling to hold this truth, then find it in others who know you. They will be able to remind you of your strength.

FIRST STEPS ON THE JOURNEY

After a miscarriage or stillbirth, please allow yourself time to heal, both physically and emotionally. We often want to rush through the healing process, believing that if we can "just get over it," we will be better. We are tired of feeling sad. But rushing through and trying to put our pain aside do not eliminate the pain. We can't will away our pain. Allow yourself all the time you need. There is no timeline. Don't compare your loss with that of others. This is your journey.

Time may feel like the enemy. Days will feel like they take forever, and you might wonder when you will feel normal or better.

Allow yourself grace and patience through this process.

Physical Healing

Although a woman may look healthy right away, healing from a miscarriage can take anywhere from a week to several weeks. Cramping is expected and can last a few days, and bleeding can last up to a week. According to the March of Dimes, depending on how far along the pregnancy was, it can take up to two months for hormones to return to their previous levels.[1] This can result in mood swings and sleep loss. The body can also feel physically tired, as if you are carrying a wet blanket. All of this is normal.

Women who have endured a stillbirth have gone through either a natural delivery or a C-section. Postpartum healing will be different depending on how you delivered your child. The seriousness of a C-section is often minimized; it is major surgery and introduces significant trauma to the body.

If you've had a C-section, you can expect to stay in the hospital for three to four days after surgery, and then healing continues for about four to six weeks. The incision will require time to heal and may cause some physical pain. You may experience fatigue on top of grief. Remember that your body is healing not only from surgery but also from pregnancy. Postpartum hormonal shifts are expected.

If you were able to have a natural childbirth, you will be sore, and the perineum will need time to heal, especially if stitches were necessary. Sitz baths and warm water sprays can help ease discomfort. Hot showers will help with aching muscles and joints.

The physical healing will take longer than you want it to. Many women want to quickly return to life as usual, but the physical limitations don't allow for that. Those limitations will feel unfair, and the pain will be a constant reminder of what has been lost. Please be aware of your feelings. Recognize your frustration when you believe the healing is taking too long. Be honest with yourself and then allow your body what it needs.

Following your doctor's advice is important while healing from delivery. Please attend your follow-up doctor's appointments.

Adding another layer to the healing process is that your body doesn't know the baby died. While parents spend the nine months leading up to a baby's arrival setting up a nursery, reading childcare books, and purchasing supplies, the mother's body spends that time preparing for delivery and aftercare. God created women's bodies not only to birth children but to nourish them as well by producing milk, whether the baby is around or not. Your body carried your baby during pregnancy and believes it still has a job to do. Having the milk come in is a painful time for baby-loss moms. While you wait for your milk to dry up, your breasts will likely be sore. Take extra precaution to be gentle. Please don't discount the physical and emotional impact this change will have. It will be yet another reminder of losing your child, and for some, how your body betrayed you. You were supposed to be able to feed your baby, and now you have the milk but no baby.

A few practices can help dry up the milk. Sometimes doctors prescribe medication to do this, while other women allow time to pass. In some cases, women use cold cabbage leaves placed against their breasts. The cabbage leaves absorb some fluid from the glands in the breast area, helping reduce engorgement.

A Memorial Service or Funeral

While your body is recovering, often while still in the hospital, you may be asked to think about a funeral or memorial service. Unless your baby had already received a terminal diagnosis in utero, this is not the planning you thought you would be doing.

Even though this process may be painful, memorials can be a lovely tribute to your child. This can be a time to honor who your child was and who they were supposed to be. Many families feel a closeness to their child in this intimate setting with loved ones around. Some also find comfort in thanking God for the gift of their child through a memorial service.

Other families choose not to have a service. Some want to move forward in the healing process privately or feel that a traditional service is unnecessary. Still other families prefer a more intimate way to honor their children that feels natural to them. As I mentioned in the previous chapter, some families plant a tree. Others participate in a toy drive.

There is no right or wrong way to honor your child. This decision is yours. Moving forward is an individual process, and you shouldn't feel shame in whatever decision you make.

I will offer one final word of advice: If you find that you are avoiding having a service because of what others will think, please remember that this is not for them; it is for you. There is nothing wrong with forgoing a service because it will bring you more pain than peace, but if others' opinions are keeping you from it, don't let their potential discomfort rob you of this experience.

If you are privileged enough to be invited to one of these services, please don't allow your discomfort to get in the way of honoring the child. Make it a priority to attend. Of course it will feel sad; please go anyway. This is an opportunity to support the child-loss parents and show them the value of their child.

Siblings

If you have other children at home, you are left in the position to help them understand and grieve. It's okay to allow children to see your true feelings. Please don't feel the need to protect them from seeing your sadness and tears. Seeing adults cry does not have to be scary for kids. They will find it more frightening if their parents aren't congruent. You might try to hide your tears, but they will still know something is upsetting you. If they ask what's wrong, answer them honestly. Children thrive when they witness a parent's honest emotions and healing.

Explaining the situation may not be easy. It can be difficult to balance honesty with kid-appropriate language and to hold their grief while managing your own.

The conversations about their sibling won't end with the hospital stay. Kids will want to talk about their sibling. They will have questions. These valuable moments can bring real connection and healing.

Children will ask the same questions you ask. They want to know what happened just as much as you do, and you still won't have answers. This will be infuriating for them and you. Your kids will see you cry, and that's okay. Parents often believe that if their kids see them cry, they will be scared. Parents are role models for kids. Kids learn emotional health from their parents, and crying is part of that. When you feel the tears coming, give yourself the freedom to cry. Don't reserve them just for in the shower.

Be honest with your kids. Let them know you are sad and that they can be sad too. Don't feel the need to hide. Kids feel the emptiness in the house; put words to it for them. Just as you might not want someone trying to take away your pain, don't feel the need to take away your child's sadness.

It is not uncommon for parents to find their kids pretending to play with their sibling. A few years ago, I worked with a mom to a four-year-old daughter and whose second daughter was given a terminal diagnosis at delivery. They spent their short time as a family of four creating memories to hold on to. Only a few months later, her second daughter died.

In the weeks after this tragedy, the mom overheard her four-year-old talking with someone in her room. When asked, her daughter explained that she was playing house with her sister. It was a touching moment for my client.

Other children draw pictures of their families that include their siblings. Sometimes these pictures are then shared at school. This sometimes creates some discomfort for a teacher, who may suggest that it might be too much for the other children in the classroom. If this happens to you, talk with the teacher. It is important to remember that the child is bringing others into their world. They want to share their sibling with people.

Pretend play is normal behavior for a child. There is no need to interrupt their play. Their imagination is an excellent tool to help them heal through their loss. Whereas adults usually communicate and process verbally, children tend to communicate through their play. Violet Oaklander, a well-known child psychotherapist and author, suggests that through play and art, children will show their inner world. In her book, *Windows to Our Children*, she states, "We can look into the inner realms of the child's being through fantasy. We can bring out what is kept hidden or avoided and we can also find out what's going on in the child's life from her perspective."[2]

Recognize whether this behavior makes you uncomfortable. Does it stir up something you would rather shut down? I encourage you to take part in your child's game if invited. Of course, it is also okay to sit out of the game if participating feels too raw for you. Sitting out does not make you a bad parent, nor will it impact your child. But if you are able to participate, ask them questions. What a great moment to honor your lost child by inviting them into play.

Marking Time

In the period immediately following a loss, many baby-loss moms begin to count the days since their baby died. For many, this feels like a morbid thing to do, and they believe it means they are not moving forward. But numbering each day is normal and won't last forever. The day you realize you are no longer counting can be sad. This does not mean your child is left behind or forgotten. When you stop counting the days, other time markers will become more prominent, such as anniversaries and holidays.

After friends and family have returned to their lives, a period of quiet settles in. In that time, the shock and numbness begin to wear off, and you may feel unsettled as you spend more time alone. The sadness might feel heavier than it did, and you may become restless trying to quiet your thoughts. This is a time to reconnect with yourself.

This period often arrives sometime between delivering your child and returning to what life was before (work and career, parenting other children, or social engagements). These are quiet moments you will want to fill with noise. They could come first thing in the morning when you wake up or midafternoon when the day is dragging. You will probably look for ways to shut yourself off from the pain through mindless television, sleep, or online shopping.

In these times, if you can begin to allow your feelings in, you will slowly start to trust them and trust yourself to manage them. Rather than immediately turning to your vice to shut down your feelings, allow them to linger for just a few minutes (sometimes seconds). The more you can let the emotions show up and lean into them, the stronger you will become and the more you can begin to feel secure, finding comfort in believing that the feelings won't be too big to handle.

In the days after Abby's death, after the chaos, I spent

a good deal of time switching between watching mindless TV and allowing my sadness to flood me. One day during a phone call, a trusted friend explained that she was concerned I wasn't dealing with my pain and that I wasn't allowing myself to feel all of it. She hadn't been with me during my days, and she was unaware of how I was spending my time. I don't know what brought her to that conclusion, but the comment hurt. I became defensive, and I didn't ask why she said that. I thought, *How could she even begin to understand what I am or am not dealing with?* In her defense, she lived out of state, and we didn't see each other enough.

I explained to her that if I allowed all the pain I was feeling to overtake me, I would wither. I would have curled up in a corner and never left.

Allowing moments of awareness is essential, but I also hold true that we need to take breaks from experiencing all the emotions. It is healthier to allow what we can handle, step away from the feelings for a time, and then allow more. This builds incremental strength so we can eventually let bigger emotions linger.

So I allowed time to sit with my emotions. Then when they became too overwhelming, I took a break, often with mindless TV. This allowed my brain to shut down my thoughts, giving me small, needed breaks from my sadness.

Leaning into the Pain

The first step in the process of leaning into the pain is to become aware.

When the trauma initially happens, the body's response is often to become numb to physical sensations. Take some time, maybe only a moment, and ask yourself, *Besides the physical healing, what physical sensations am I feeling?* Is there a tightness in your chest? Is your stomach queasy? Are these sensations new, or have you experienced them before?

These could be your body's way of letting you know you are feeling sad or angry. Take a moment to breathe and notice if you are trying to push those feelings away. It's not uncommon to try to suppress those emotions.

If you discover that you are trying to run from your emotions, I'm going to ask you to sit. Take a moment to rest. If you're home, find your favorite spot in the house. Feel the chair beneath you—or the floor if you are using it—and just sit. Maybe close your eyes and breathe in and out. If you can allow yourself a few minutes, just breathe.

While you are breathing, focus only on each breath. Give your brain a moment without any thoughts running through it. Breathe in and out. If it's difficult to do this, count in for three seconds and out for three seconds.

Do this for two minutes. What do you feel? Are the physical sensations you noticed before still with you? If you are feeling some sadness, can you allow it to linger? Do you need to fill time and give yourself a break from feeling anything? Is it challenging to quiet your mind? Was two minutes too long? Can you do it for one minute?

Allow yourself the opportunity to recognize what is going on in you. Lean into the moment, and let the feelings be known and felt. Is leaning into your sadness too much for you right now? There is no right or wrong answer. If so, allow space for that to be okay for now. If it doesn't feel right to do this now, come back to it later.

When you are ready, come back to this spot to sit in your emotions. I know finding time to lean into your sadness can be challenging, especially if you have children at home. I still encourage you to find moments to practice this behavior. I also know that most of you reading this book are tired of feeling sad. But the more you can allow a feeling, the less the emotion will fight to be heard, lessening its grip on you.

A commonly held misconception is that if we allow ourselves to wallow in negative emotions, we will get stuck. We believe that if we start crying, we will never stop. That's not true. Have you ever noticed that when you try to ignore an emotion, it shows up anyway? Sometimes it rears its head in the most unlikely ways, like hives. The more you resist a feeling, the harder it will try to push through.

If we try to avoid our emotional pain, physical symptoms may appear. In the realm of mental health, this is labeled as somatization: the unconscious process of psychological distress manifesting as physical symptoms.

We often make allowances for other people's pain, but when it comes to our own pain, we tend to run away from it. We shove it as far down as possible and put on a smile. If this is your pattern, I encourage you to take a moment to consider why this is. Ask yourself, *Why do I run from my own pain?*

I realize the simplest answer is that you don't want to be sad. I've heard that many times. I want to challenge you with this: whether you like it or not, you are sad. You feel sad even if you say you're not. And even if you have moments of happiness, you will be sad again. Having feelings is part of the human condition, and one of those feelings is sadness. Trying to push away the sadness does not work. Allowing the sadness the time it deserves (yes, sadness deserves a moment) can bring about healing. Give yourself the gift of honoring your emotions.

There may come a time when you lean into the emotions and they feel overwhelming. The waves of sadness crash against your soul at a pace you can't take anymore. That's a great time to allow your brain to shut down.

That may be a time to watch mindless TV or read a good book. As I said earlier, I binge-watched seasons of pointless television. I didn't have the emotional energy to read, and I knew my mind wouldn't shut down while reading a book. I needed something mindless. For some, this is a moment to leave the house and find new scenery. Take a walk with your earbuds in and listen to music.

Sometimes the best thing we can do for ourselves is to allow the brain some downtime.

Many people find healing in meditation and prayer. A sense of peace may be found if we allow the space to quiet our minds, focusing on the presence of God. The psalmist writes in Psalm 119:76–77,

> Let your steadfast love comfort me
>> according to your promise to your servant.
> Let your mercy come to me, that I may live;
>> for your law is my delight.

If, however, your mind will not quiet, then this may not be the time to sit silently, and that's okay. Don't try to force a moment. There will be more opportunities.

But if and when you are ready, I encourage you to find

a place where you feel God's presence, such as your garden, a cozy chair, or somewhere in nature. Make sure this place feels peaceful to you in your current emotional state. Find a passage of Scripture that feels healing and meditate on it. Allow God to speak to you, and give yourself the gift of being honest with him.

Remember, it is okay if you find it challenging to stay in that space for any length of time. God understands where you are. He sees you, and he knows your heart. Allow him to come alongside you.

If it is challenging to find a space that feels comfortable, that's okay too. If all you can do is hold to the promise that God is present, then hold tight. God will be there when you are ready.

ADDRESSING THE NURSERY

Most people set up a nursery for the arrival of their little one, and if not a nursery, some space for the baby. Furniture is bought, strollers are assembled, and clothes are washed and put away.

Facing the question of what to do with these things can be daunting. These things were bought with love and anticipation, and now they are shards of glass in a gaping wound, creating pain every time you take a breath.

The thoughtful offers of help from friends to help donate or find homes for the items can contribute to the pain. These offers are kind and filled with much care, but that doesn't make them hurt any less. It is a struggle to imagine giving away your baby's things before you've come to grips with the notion that your baby won't need them.

There is no hard-and-fast rule for when or if you should redo the baby's room. There is no harm in leaving the room the way it is open-endedly. When you are ready, you can decide what is next for that space and the baby's things. Some families choose to allow the room to stay as is, with the clothes, the furniture, and the toys left in their places for years. They find comfort in leaving the room unchanged. It can be their place to "sit with" their child and find a connection.

I worked with a couple that came in for guidance in helping their daughter who suffered a stillbirth. It had been a few months, and they were concerned because they had learned that their daughter would sleep in her son's crib: "Not every night, but she does take naps there." This made them worry that she was stuck in her grief. Please hear this: it is normal to sleep in your baby's crib. And there is nothing abnormal about grabbing a blanket and sleeping in the rocking chair that was supposed to be your child's. This behavior does not mean anyone is stuck or not grieving well. Women long to be near their children, and some find comfort in the crib. That is okay.

Not every family chooses to keep the nursery as it is. Some choose to turn that room into something else or leave it for any subsequent children. If you choose to remove the baby's things immediately, I encourage you to hold on to a keepsake. This is a tangible way to hold on to your child. This decision is personal, and again, there is no right or wrong choice.

Leaving Home

When it is time to return to life outside the home, please allow for grace and compassion for yourself. We often believe that we will be returning to the same thing we left, but that is often untrue.

Returning to work can often be a welcome distraction. It brings about structure and a new focus besides grief. The brain can now concentrate on something in familiar surroundings. Work also allows for some casual social interactions.

For many, returning to work can be difficult. It is not uncommon for the work atmosphere to look the same but feel different. Please don't try to return before you're ready. As in the case of trying to hurry your physical healing, you don't want to rush back to your old normal. It is no longer an option. You now live in a new normal.

Returning to work could be the first time you come face-to-face with difficult ongoing questions: *How do I interact with others when I am not the same? Am I going to have to retell the story again in public?* Here, compassion and grace will be essential. Give yourself permission to excuse yourself from a conversation, if necessary. Get some fresh air if you need it, or hole up in a closed office or closet. Build boundaries around what is comfortable for you in interactions with others.

If you need to return to work earlier than you would like, be extra kind to yourself before and after your workday. Allow more time to breathe deeply, and maybe drink an extra cup of coffee. Perhaps you need a few additional minutes of sleep. Give yourself what you need to be a good employee, but first and foremost, be kind to you.

This is a great time to practice listening to what your gut is telling you. You may anticipate that preloss conversations will feel the same now, but sometimes they don't. There's no need to push through, telling yourself that if you can't stay in the conversation you are too emotional or weak. Remember, there is a new element to who you are now. This may feel unfair because you didn't ask for this change, but regardless, you are different from who you were. That's why you must be more attentive to yourself than normal; you are learning to navigate the world in a new way.

Returning to social outings can also be challenging. Until you feel comfortable, choose to hang out only with safe people. This may seem unhealthy to some, as if you are avoiding life. But selecting safe people allows you to practice in social situations, and it gives you time to build new boundaries.

Sometimes our safe people turn out to be people outside our family, making family gatherings challenging. If this is true for you, please know you have options. The least comfortable option—but still an option—may be setting a boundary to avoid family for a time. I know this may sound hard. If this is not possible for you, then it is best to enter these situations with a buffer, such as a husband, friend, or trusted family member. Agree to a time frame before you arrive at the gathering, and plan out how and when you will leave.

If you're a friend of someone who recently experienced child loss or a miscarriage, flexibility is key. Safe friendships are built on a foundation of compassion and understanding. For baby-loss parents, sometimes it is hard to pull the trigger and leave the house. They will need grace and support from you to know that the need to stay home is not about anything or anyone except their own heart. Remind yourself that if your friend cancels plans and doesn't want to go out, that doesn't mean you have a bad relationship. On the contrary, if you stay flexible in those situations, you show that your relationship is a safe one.

QUESTIONS FOR REFLECTION

If you've experienced a miscarriage or stillbirth, what did you find helpful while healing physically?

If you've experienced child loss while raising other children, what has been challenging in parenting those siblings?

What is a tangible way you have found to hold on to your child?

Chapter 4

AM I CRAZY?

In most situations, when women discover they are pregnant, their immediate response is to begin taking care of their child and their health. They do this in many ways, including proper nutrition and doctor's visits. As their belly continues to grow, they begin talking and singing to their child. They give their child a name and an identity. Parents plan around who they hope their child will be, what schools they will attend, who their friends might be, and what their personality might be like.

For those who experience miscarriage or child loss, these plans are taken away in an instant. Instead, parents are left with "I didn't get to say goodbye." But losing a child during pregnancy is more than just a sad goodbye. It is a traumatic loss that impacts a woman's whole body, including the brain.

Bessel van der Kolk has spent his over-thirty-year career researching and treating trauma and is considered one of the leading experts in the field. In his book, *The Body Keeps the Score*, Van der Kolk states, "Trauma results in a fundamental reorganization of the way mind and brain manage perceptions. It changes not only how we think and what we think about, but also our very capacity to think."[1]

He described three things that occur during an experience of trauma.[2]

First, trauma creates a fear-driven brain by enhancing the threat perception system. The traumatized brain sees danger where others see manageable situations.

Remember when I mentioned that my brain shifted when I heard the news that there was no heartbeat? I felt as if I had dissociated; my brain was disconnecting from my mind and body, and at the same time, my mind went into overdrive. This happened because my brain had just suffered a trauma.

At that moment, my brain shifted into a fear-driven brain. My mind started to see danger all around me. Everything became unknown and scary. It felt like dissociation, which can happen when a person doesn't feel safe. The brain disconnects from the present. The mind looks for refuge.

Dissociation is the process of disconnecting from thoughts, feelings, memories, and sometimes a sense of identity. It is often a subconscious process that we aren't aware of. Others recognize it but are unsure why it is happening. Some people describe it as if their brain just went black; there was no thought. Have you ever been in a situation, feeling bored or maybe doing some sort of rote task at work, and you find yourself daydreaming? Or your brain shifts its thinking, and you can't grab on to any thought? That could be dissociation. Whereas daydreaming can occur out of boredom, dissociation is common during a traumatic situation.

Second, Van der Kolk suggests that trauma impacts the brain's filtering system. The mind can't distinguish between what is essential and what isn't. Information that before the trauma felt superfluous now becomes important. Because the filtering system is impeded, it can't hold on to what is important and let go of what isn't. Every piece of information is taken in. In my case, it became nearly impossible to stay present.

Third, trauma numbs the self-sensing system. In the body's defense against the overwhelming feelings of the trauma, the brain works to numb itself. It numbs not only the overwhelming sadness and fear but the feelings of love and security as well.

In the moment of trauma, our brains go into survival mode. They work to keep us safe by actively searching for a perceived threat. Our minds work to take in all valuable information while on high alert for danger, and we numb our emotions. This happens on top of the other physical traumas of delivery right as we are saying goodbye to our child.

We must be aware of how the brain is impacted, because we operate differently after intense trauma. Our actions may feel different. When others are looking for us to fall apart, we may look apathetic. This could be confusing for those around us.

Trauma permeates not only our physical and emotional healing but also our relationships with ourselves and others, which we will discuss further in the following chapters.

"We have learned that trauma is not just an event that took place sometime in the past; it is also the imprint left by that experience on the mind, brain, and body," writes Van der Kolk in *The Body Keeps the Score*. "For real change [healing] to take place, the body needs to learn that the danger has passed and to live in the reality of the present."[3]

Women who believe they "should be over it by now" don't realize how much their loss has changed them. Feelings of pain and strong emotion seem to come out of nowhere, but they are lingering effects of the trauma they have experienced. Van der Kolk suggests that after a woman has experienced the trauma of losing a child, her mind and body believe they are still under attack. As the days progress and the brain begins to feel safe again, grief starts to find its place.

The challenge for baby-loss moms is that it's not obvious when safety has been achieved. The danger seems to lie within their own body. For example, women who have suffered a previous loss feel powerful fear and anxiety when taking subsequent pregnancy tests. Other women are confused when they aren't "as excited as they should be" at the news of a pregnancy.

FINDING SAFETY

Because the brain is healing, the effects of trauma can linger beyond what feels like an appropriate time. You may believe your brain fog and fatigue should resolve quicker than they do. You might be tempted to base your healing journey on things you read online or conversations you have with people. But each journey is different. Please don't compare yours with someone else's. Remember, there is no "normal" time frame for healing. As your brain begins to feel safe, you will start to heal from the trauma.

Coping skills you have used for difficult situations in the past may not work for you now. This is a new journey for you.

Don't be surprised if the way you previously dealt with loss doesn't work in this new territory. And, just to be clear, trauma and grief are two separate things. On the other side of the trauma, the grief is still waiting.

In this journey toward a new feeling of safety, where we believe that bad things don't happen daily, allow yourself time to heal physically. Too often women are tempted to hurry through the physical healing from the trauma the body has just endured. But in the case of stillbirth or miscarriage, it is even more vital that we give our bodies what they need to heal. We can't expect to walk the emotional journey without a physical reserve.

Many baby-loss moms attribute their fatigue to the trauma the body just endured, and that is true. If surgery is part of your delivery story, your body is working to heal itself. The natural delivery of a child and the physical aspects of miscarriage are also exhausting. But we can't ignore that grief is also a significant contributor to fatigue.

When I say fatigue, I'm talking about the bone-tired, I'm-carrying-a-one-thousand-pound-boulder fatigue. You will feel exhausted. I encourage you not to muscle through this. This is not mind over matter or the time to shame yourself into not being tired. This is a time to rest.

You may find in the early days of grief that you want to sleep all the time. Or you may not sleep at all. Both are typical responses to grief. If you aren't sleeping because your mind won't quiet, find a journal or notebook to keep by your bed. It can be helpful to write down the thoughts that won't stop looping through your brain. When you write them down, put the journal away and tell yourself you no longer need to think those thoughts because they are safely written down and you can go back to them later.

Journaling isn't a good fit for everyone. (I'm not a good journaler.) But this isn't necessarily about journaling. The journal by the bed could be designated for brain dumps only. If you choose, sometime later read what you wrote. If you don't want to read it, then don't.

Nightmares are common during this time, and it is natural to relive the trauma through those dreams. That can feel unfair. We have already done this once; why do we have to keep reliving it? The subconscious is doing its job to help you heal. Sometimes your dreams won't make sense. Please don't look for meaning in them. You will not find in your dreams the answer to why your baby died.

Women I have had the privilege to work with often come into my office and share a dream that they want to hold truth for them. The dream is often interpreted this way: "I'm going to be sick and die, and God didn't want my baby to live without me." This gives a grieving mom some comfort in that they have found a reason for the loss, but I have yet to meet someone who got sick after one of these dreams.

Friends may also have dreams about your baby. These dreams often involve seeing or interacting with your baby a few months old. Other dreams lead the friend to some resolution of how you will come to be a parent to a future child. These dreams can hold comfort for a grieving parent.

Some feelings may arise as a result of a dream. These feelings are valid, so please don't discount them. Allow them to be what they are. Don't push them aside or minimize them because they came as a result of a dream.

It is also common for moms to wake up from their dreams and nightmares looking for their child. It can be frightening for the other person in the bed with you to hear you calling for your child. Sometimes moms get up and go down the hall looking for their child. (They may or may not be fully awake.) Although it is heartbreaking not to find your baby, this behavior does not make you crazy. It is a typical way of dealing with the trauma of this loss.

If sleep is elusive and you don't know why, then sleep when you can. Grief doesn't stick to a schedule, so you shouldn't expect to either. If you are sleeping too much, then in the moments when you are awake, go outside. Sit in your yard and breathe. If being quiet is not the right choice for you, then find something to listen to. Go on a walk (assuming your doctor clears you to do so). If you don't have the energy for a walk, I still encourage you to spend some time in the sun, since that can help with sadness.

The body needs sleep to heal, and when we are tired, our emotions feel more intense. You need rest. Some people find that a routine helps prepare them to sleep. Going to sleep and getting up at the same time every night can work too. Some find quietness helps them drift off, while others prefer some noise. There's no harm in using mindless TV or a podcast to fall asleep. And what worked for you yesterday may not work today. If not, then look for something new.

During the early days, you may experience brain fog. You may become more forgetful and have moments of memory loss. It isn't unusual to forget whether you ate, what you did during the day, or what day it is. Your body is going through a hormonal shift as well as grief, and this can impact your memory. You are not crazy, and you are not alone. The brain is working to incorporate the grief, so thoughts perceived as "extra" may be overlooked. But this won't always be the case.

Van der Kolk suggests, "Traumatized people need to learn that they can tolerate their sensations, befriend their inner experiences, and cultivate new action patterns."[4] Only with time, rest, and healing will your brain start to sense a return to safety after this intense trauma.

ANXIETY

Many women begin to experience anxiety in the time following a loss. For some, this is their first experience with it. For others, the stress builds on what was already there. Anxiety can often be felt as a physical sensation somewhere in the body. Some feel it as a heaviness in their chest, others feel a flutter in their stomach, and others feel a tingle in their arms.

Still others find that their anxiety plays out with their minds ruminating on thoughts that won't leave. Their mind is working to fix the situation. Some women find themselves wondering about the future and subsequent pregnancies. This creates fear and more anxiety. As I've mentioned frequently, I encourage you to work toward quieting your mind. Remind yourself to stay in the present, focus on today, and even focus on this moment.

In the immediate, remember that breathing exercises can help to soothe your anxious mind. Take deeper breaths. If you find that you can't breathe deeply, then work to slow your breathing.

During moments of more intense anxiety or when you

recognize the fear, take a deep breath in for three counts, hold for three counts, and breathe out for three counts. If this doesn't work to relieve some of the anxiety, then change your scenery. Move from one spot to another, go outside, take a walk.

To reduce anxiety, some people find it helpful to take a moment to ground themselves. Sometimes just feeling the ground beneath you is enough. Find a comfortable spot in your home, plant both feet on the ground, and feel the ground with all four corners of your feet. Sometimes it is more grounding to sit against something solid, like a wall or a tree. Concentrate on feeling the solidness behind you and the ground beneath you.

Another great way to feel grounded is to take a barefoot walk. Walking barefoot allows for a different connection to the ground than with shoes on. I know that most people might not want to go walking barefoot down their sidewalk, so if you have the opportunity, drive to a park and walk barefoot in the grass. Feeling the sand with your toes at the beach can also bring a sense of grounding. I encourage you to find a place to walk barefoot. Allow yourself to connect to the ground beneath you.

Scent is a tool that can be helpful but is often overlooked. Lavender can be a great fragrance to create a calming environment, whereas citrus is a good scent to uplift a mood. If a certain scent creates calm or a feeling of warmth for you, diffuse it. This can help create a grounding space for you in your home. Some women have found it helpful to carry the scent on them, such as putting it on their wrist.

If that isn't enough, then I encourage the 5, 4, 3, 2, 1

method. Before you follow these steps, please take a moment to breathe in and then breathe out.

Acknowledge five things you see: "I see a sofa. I see a cup," and so on.

Acknowledge four things you feel: "I feel my feet on the ground. I feel the sofa I am sitting on," and so on.

Acknowledge three things you hear: "I hear the dog barking, I hear a car horn, and I hear the clock ticking."

Acknowledge two things you smell: "I smell the coffee from this morning. I smell the flowers outside." If you need to search out these smells, that's okay.

Acknowledge one thing you can taste: "I taste the sandwich I'm eating for lunch."

When you have completed the steps, take another moment to breathe, both in and out.

Work toward keeping yourself connected to the present. Grounding practices, such as the activity we just went through, can help anxiety. You may have to tell yourself to stop the anxious thoughts and to stay in the present. It can be challenging to do so if you are actively trying to figure out the future, if we are continually trying to fix the problem. We have no control over the outcome, and we work to control what we have no control over. But the sadness will not go away by coming up with a fix to the problem, because we don't know what that is. There is often no fix to the problem.

If you find it difficult to stop your thoughts from swirling in your brain, I encourage wearing a rubber band around your wrist. Some women find a hair band works, but a rubber band works best. When you find that the thoughts won't stop, gently snap the rubber band against your wrist. It will sting a bit and will not stop your anxiety completely. This technique is in no way meant to cause pain or self-harm. It is intended only to create a second for your thoughts to stop. I encourage you then, in the moment, to shift your thinking to something else. Find a thought that you can always come back to, such as the time the dog did something funny or what you had for dinner last night.

Recognize the things you do have control over, and take ownership of those. We have control over what we eat. We can control what we wear and choose to watch or read. We mostly have control over who we talk to in a day. Many believe we have control over our feelings. That is not true. We only have control over what we do with those feelings.

Many people find that yoga is a great way to get back in touch with their bodies. Yoga allows participants to learn how their breath connects to their body. It brings awareness of the feelings in the body and how the body moves. This can sound intimidating to some, or maybe a bit too new agey. If yoga is something you would like to try, make sure your doctor approves. Find a yoga studio that feels comfortable, and if you want, bring a friend.

Sometimes when movement happens, the muscles release emotion, and we find ourselves crying. We don't have words to explain why we are crying, and it often takes us by surprise. This can make you feel out of control. Crying can be a cathartic release. Embrace the tears. Like other aspects of grief and trauma we've discussed, this response is normal. You are not crazy.

You may find that you sometimes eat more than usual—"feeding your emotions"—or not wanting to eat at all. Both of these responses are typical. If you can, please feed your body.

Staying hydrated will help with the fatigue. This is not the time to try a new food plan or to start a diet.

If you're caring for someone who experienced child loss, this isn't the time to fight with them to eat. Unless someone is manifesting physical symptoms of malnutrition, telling them "you need to" isn't the answer. I know it can be scary to watch someone struggle, but fighting someone or guilting them into something doesn't work. If you are seriously concerned about their health, then contact a doctor for guidance.

Journaling can be a useful practice. Unlike the brain dump, this is where you can journal whatever you want to write about. Whatever you write is for you and you alone, unless you want to share it with others. Some women find it helpful to write to their child, others write to God, and still others journal whatever happened during that day.

Keep in mind that journaling does not work for everyone. If you try to force it, journaling can create more anxiety.

If you choose to journal, don't concern yourself with proper grammar and punctuation. This is not a place for appropriateness; it is a place to be raw and open. You can be as messy as you want. And don't worry about becoming "good" at journaling. There will be no grading. This is just for you.

If the anxiety is difficult to manage on your own, then please reach out for help. If the fear is not subsiding, or is growing, please seek advice. This may be a great time to seek counseling or speak with your doctor. Many excellent group counseling services are offered through hospitals and churches. Many baby-loss families find comfort in these settings. Please don't feel that the grief and anxiety are something you need to carry on your own.

Van der Kolk says in *The Body Keeps the Score*, "At the core of recovery is self-awareness."[5] The journey isn't about overcoming grief as if pain were a disorder. The journey is allowing the grief to become part of who we are. It becomes part of our self-awareness, and we begin to feel safe again in the process.

When we, even in the pit of sadness, can breathe in and breathe out and lean into the pain, knowing it won't kill us, this is where recovery begins. This is where we learn we can trust ourselves. This is where we learn that we are safe.

QUESTIONS FOR REFLECTION

Have you experienced dissociation during a traumatic moment? If so, what was that like for you?

Where do you feel safe and calm?

Do you find healing in keeping a journal? Why or why not?

Chapter 5

SHIFTING RELATIONSHIPS

After the death of a child, many women don't anticipate the dramatic changes in their relationships. As I mentioned in the previous chapter, trauma creates an internal change. Because of this, our relationships with ourselves, family, friends, and God shift as well.

Relationships continually grow and evolve. When a traumatic loss occurs, it shifts a person instantly and intensely. Relationships have no option but to adjust or run the risk of ending altogether.

No Return to Normal

When I was recouping from my C-section at the hospital, I couldn't wait to get back to the safety of home. I expected to return to my old life as the same person who drove to the hospital, minus my child. But my house no longer felt like my home. It was unfamiliar. My perception had shifted, and the world became scary. My home no longer felt safe because I didn't feel safe inside my body.

My inability to navigate familiar surroundings was due to my shocked state. This was my brain working to keep me safe, but it resulted in yet another unanticipated challenge. When I went to the hospital, I had been preparing myself to navigate life with a newborn. When I left, I found myself relearning how to do things that had always been second nature.

Families that have said goodbye to their children see life differently than before. One of the most significant shifts is that we experience an emotional depth that others may never know. I don't believe it is possible to dwell in such deep grief without creating the pathway to a new depth of emotion. We then experience the world through this new lens. Over time, experiencing life on a deeper level can become a gift. But in the throes of this sadness, it feels like a curse. It feels unfair and painful. And it is.

This new place can feel terrifying. We no longer trust the things that we used to have faith in, such as the confidence of waking up and believing the day will go as planned. And because we don't feel secure in that foundation, we don't know how to imagine the future. We may remain hyperaware of the "what ifs": *How do I protect what I have no control over? How do I plan for the future when I have no say in what happens?*

Finding our way back from this loss takes time. It always takes longer than we want, and at times the grief will feel unending. I encourage you to continue taking step after step. Breathe in and out, even when you don't want to. It takes time to become familiar with the new you.

Allow yourself some time to learn what feels good right now. Having dinner in your favorite restaurant will probably have a different feel. Even when you are with your most beloved person, this restaurant may no longer hold the same appeal, or your favorite meal could become tasteless. Driving the same route to the grocery store may look different. Nights out with the girls won't be the same. Conversations that came naturally before your loss may feel unnatural for a while. That's okay; it won't always be like that.

These changes don't mean you are losing your mind, nor are you broken. If past experiences no longer feel good, then search for new ones. There is no harm in finding a new route to work or shopping at a new grocery store. No rule says the things you held close before your loss need to be held on to now.

Also, the familiarity of these situations and places may come back after some time. If you want to hold on to what was, then hold on. If not, find something new. If you want to continue having dinner at your old favorite restaurant, hoping that the familiarity comes back, then do so. If not, then find a new favorite. There is no right or wrong approach to navigating the newness.

As I've mentioned in previous chapters, you will often wonder if you are stuck in your grief. You will question yourself, or others will ask you why things aren't better yet. Remember, this is uncharted territory and not a linear process. You won't get stuck in your pain. Please give yourself the time needed.

This journey is not a sprint to get over the loss. It is an internalization of the experience and the moments along the way. Take the time to experience yourself as you are, lean into the pain, and grow in ways you didn't know you could.

If you are a friend or loved one of a child-loss parent, please avoid placing a time limit on their grief. The road is different for everyone. Sometimes the need to know that a friend is healed is more about trying to go back to the way things were. But things will never again be the way they were for that parent. Recognize their need, and make room for something new.

After the loss of a child, our friends and family will experience us differently. We may look the same externally, but internally we are transformed. The ease of relationships may shift, and the rules may change. What the relationship was before is no longer. That doesn't have to be a bad thing. It can create the opportunity to have a deeper and sometimes more rewarding relationship.

Shifting Friendships

In my experience working with baby-loss moms, it is a joy to hear of relationships that still flourish. These are the stories of friends who learned to navigate the newness. The path may start off rocky but end up leading to cherished lifelong friendships.

I also know of friendships that ended. This is something no one intends. It often comes out of the blue and leaves confusion and hurt in the wake.

Many things can strain a friendship, but two that are likely to end one are unintentionally hurtful words and comparisons of loss. There are many names for unintentionally hurtful words: platitudes, uplifting texts, advice, and comparisons. These words are spoken to help alleviate the pain. All baby-loss moms have heard them. They are spoken in love but received in pain.

Women who have suffered a miscarriage don't want to hear sage advice. Moms who have had to bury their child don't want platitudes or guidance. Bereaved moms don't want comparisons to other forms of loss or that "it will get better with time."

Although the intention of these words is compassion, they don't deliver that message. Frequently that intention is lost in the translation, and the words fall flat. But they don't fall on deaf ears. What was meant to be sincere is received as minimizing and hurtful, and these words get caught up in the loop. The bereaved parents are left feeling even more depleted.

There is also a chance the bereaved parent is left feeling guilty as a result of this exchange. They want to hear the compassion in what was spoken. On an intellectual level, they know the words weren't meant to be hurtful, but they still feel less than settled in what was said. The guilt piles on as they think, *I shouldn't feel this way; they were just trying to help.*

The platitude "your baby is in a better place" may not be met with a warm reception. Many parents believe their baby is in heaven, but it is hard to consider that heaven is a better place for their child than in their arms. "God needed another angel" is also popular, but is that true? This statement is not a biblical truth. God created angels and then he created humans. People don't become angels after death.

"I can't even begin to imagine" is another common sentiment. Although this statement may sound good, it probably isn't. "I can't imagine what you are going through" sends the message that you don't want to understand. Here's the reality:

You can imagine what the parent is going through, but maybe you don't want to. It is too scary or sad. The perceived pain is too much to bear, so those words are said from a safe place while the grieving parent continues in their pain.

These comments are challenging for families enduring a loss. Those families don't have the emotional energy to dig through these comments to see the underlying intention. So this is what happens: A well-intentioned comment is delivered. The couple or baby-loss mom on the receiving end listens to it and takes it in without response or with a limited reply. Both parties walk away from that exchange, one believing it was a warm and loving interaction, the other is left reeling. Because there is no awareness of the pain caused, these comments may continue, creating a vicious cycle.

Rather than platitudes, I suggest starting with this: "I have no words." The baby-loss mom can understand this and hear the truth in it. "I wish it were not true" also conveys an understood truth. These are both sentiments the baby-loss mom is saying to herself. "I am sorry" also speaks truth. Sentiments that speak truth while leaving room to listen for new understanding are a gift.

Besides platitudes, comparisons of loss also fall flat. Trying to convey understanding through comparing one loss to another will never be received well. The intent may be kind, but they result in hurt and anger. I can say without hesitation that every baby-loss mom has heard a comparison of loss. Women who have suffered a stillbirth or early baby death don't want their loss to be compared to an elderly parent's death.

One client came into a session particularly hurt over her daughter's death being compared to a friend's dog passing away.

Pets are certainly family members and deserve a loving family, but as sad as it is to say goodbye to our beloved dogs or cats, their death cannot be compared to that of a daughter or son.

Please hear that my intention is not to sound harsh or shaming. I hope, through honesty, we can find a new way of interacting and create a new pathway to helping.

I remember, in a particularly emotional moment, relaying to a friend a hurtful comment I had received from someone else. I was trying to process the hurt and struggling with how to respond to those words. My friend suggested, "You just need to see the intention under the comment." But I didn't have the emotional energy to do that. My options were to leave the comment as spoken and keep holding my anger or to let the person know the pain they caused.

It is the responsibility of the baby-loss mom to acknowledge her hurt. It was my responsibility to bring up with my friend her hurtful comment. Often the energy spent grieving takes away the ability to recognize, in the moment, the full impact of the comment. The words spin around the baby-loss mom's brain, and in moments of extra anger or hurt, they are pulled out like a weapon. This can happen in a discussion with a friend, creating an argument. Or these words are layered on top of the grief, creating another layer of anger and hurt for a baby-loss mom. As a result, she feels less safe around her friend. Conversations with the friend shift, and the dynamics of the relationship change. Finally, to protect herself from more hurt, the baby-loss mom often ends the relationship.

I know this sounds unfair. I agree. Nothing is fair about any of this.

It is rare for a friendship to return to what it was if unintentionally hurtful comments continue and remain unaddressed.

The comments often continue because well-meaning friends feel the distance in the friendship. They think the relationship has shifted, they feel their friend pulling away, and they try to say the right thing to make it better. Unfortunately, the comments continue to hit at the wound, and the relationship continues to falter. Again, this is unfair.

I have seen relationships heal from this dynamic. Imagine how much more connected you could feel to someone if you had an honest conversation with them, expressed your hurt, and were heard. Imagine if you could share how the "stupid" comment made you feel, without defensiveness getting in the way.

For healing in the relationship to occur, both parties need to listen without needing to fix or defend. Feel the freedom not to have the right words and to allow silence. Recognize that although the hurtful words were intended to be loving, the end result didn't feel loving. Practice being brave and voicing the hurt. This is a great place to practice sitting and listening. Hear what is being said without working to form a response. Be patient and compassionate with each other. Be compassionate with yourself.

Maybe you just thought, *But this isn't how our relationship works.* What you mean is, this isn't how your relationship used to work. Remember, the friendship may look the same, but it isn't. It shifted when the baby died. Trauma changed the relationship. Be open to the possibility of doing things differently now. These friendships can grow and continue to be great.

We all have friends or family members who are more comfortable in a less emotional role. They often describe themselves as "just not emotional." They can be great people, always available and always wanting to make everyone smile. Sometimes we want emotional support from people like this. We hope they can give it, we share our feelings with them, and we are left disappointed or angry. Too many times we hope the person will step up for us. But if that person isn't emotionally supportive, don't keep pushing. Find that support in someone else.

Sometimes a relationship will not last. Sometimes new boundaries are established, and the friendship loses some of its closeness. These changes in a relationship add more sadness and confusion for all parties involved, creating another layer to the healing process.

Paul writes in Ephesians 4:32, "Be kind to one another, tenderhearted, forgiving one another, as God in Christ forgave you." Healing can also be found in forgiveness. If a relationship ends because it is no longer safe, please allow room for kindness and forgiveness. The friendship didn't end out of malice, and forgiveness isn't just about fixing the friendship. Recognize that although the relationship no longer works, you have the ability to see the good that you shared, hold on to memories, and move on with love in your heart.

SHIFTING MARRIAGE RELATIONSHIPS

The trauma of a baby loss or miscarriage may also impact a marriage. It can create a new and more intimate relationship or create another layer in need of healing.

Most couples I know that have suffered a traumatic loss lean on each other. Their shared experience creates a dynamic of "us against the world." There is a lot of healing in that, and it can create a unique bond.

On the other hand, hurts can build when one partner doesn't feel understood or is shut down in conversation about the experience. One partner might expect that the other perceives what they just went through in the same way. The truth is, as with anything in life, the experience will be perceived differently for everyone impacted. We see this during family vacations. A roller coaster is exhilarating to one member of the family and terrifying to another. A parent might think of a road trip as an opportunity for family bonding, while the kids in the back seat see it as a prison sentence.

A great place to start a healing conversation is by sharing about your unique experiences. Be open to hearing what it was like for your partner. You both, indeed, shared the same loss, but each of you will have a different reaction to it. Their experience might be different from yours, and that's okay. There is no need to convince them that their experience should have been something it wasn't. Be willing to share your own experience. Allow your partner to be part of your experience.

To create a healing conversation, first you must create a safe environment. Set aside preconceived notions, allow space for the unexpected, and remember that no opinion or thought is wrong. Listen without needing to respond. Be honest about your ability to listen at that moment. If you aren't able to listen right then, that's okay; just find a better time to have a conversation. This safe conversation allows for a new and more intimate understanding of your partner.

When couples find that each partner grieves differently, one person may wish the other mourned in the same manner. Or they might believe their partner isn't grieving correctly. It's common for one partner to misunderstand the grief process of the other. This road can bring about its own healing if the confused person shows patience and a desire to listen to the other's path.

If you find that hurt or resentment lingers, summon the strength to remember who your partner was before the loss. Hold on to the truth that love is there. Remember the reasons why you work as a couple. This can be daunting in the throes of grieving your baby. Can you remember your first date or the time when you first said I love you? Read an old love letter or a journal entry from a happier time. Hold on to those moments and remember those feelings.

You may need a night out. I know that might feel overwhelming and require a lot of effort, but it will likely end up being a good night. Recreate a date that left good memories, talk about nothing important, and laugh. Enjoy each other.

These roads to healing and understanding aren't fast, and many parts aren't smooth. They require energy that can be hard to come by, but in the end, these roads can lead to a more profound love for each other.

SHIFTING RELATIONSHIPS WITH FAMILY

These relationship shifts can happen in families as well. Family members who have been our biggest cheerleaders and most reliable supporters can become unsafe. Many bereaved parents find that family members want to minimize or dismiss the loss. In an attempt to help, family members often don't want to talk about it, or offer help in ways that feel invasive. They become overly attentive to perceived needs without discussing the elephant in the room. This can feel disrespectful, creating a relationship that is unsafe. A few dynamics may occur. Your parents carry not only their own feelings over losing their grandchild, but they are also worried about their own child: you. This could muddy the relationship.

Grandparents grieve their beloved grandchild. They may have been there every step of the way during the pregnancy, anxiously waiting to meet the newest member of the family. They dreamed of what this child would be and, like you, planned out the life the child would lead. They were excited to see their own child become a parent, and—who are we kidding—probably prayed for some payback after your teenage years.

These same grandparents have to watch their own child in the most profound pain they can imagine. They must manage their own pain while being there for their child. This requires great strength.

If there is a healthy parent-child relationship, parents can become their child's most significant support, allowing for a safe harbor in the healing process. Healing can be complicated if the connection is not healthy or if good boundaries haven't been established.

In some cases, the child has to become caretaker to their parents. Therapists refer to this as the "parentified child." Children who have been parentified grew up taking care of the adults in their life. Their role may have been established as a young child and was the norm for the family. This creates a lifelong pattern of caring for others and an internal message that the child is responsible for everything, including things they have no control over.

Often parentified women don't realize the pattern and struggle with layers of guilt: not being enough, their child dying, not being able to get pregnant or miscarrying, failing those around them. These feelings of guilt are lies. But because their emotional reserve is empty, these women may experience amplified versions of these feelings while healing from a loss.

Most baby-loss moms feel some guilt over their child's death. A woman who has been parentified believes, on a deep level, that she is responsible for everything that occurs, including her child dying. She also carries the sadness others are enduring and may take responsibility for that too.

Women feel guilty for "causing" this pain for their families. People outside this dynamic can see the truth: that no one caused the baby to die and no one is responsible for the pain. But parentified women grow up believing they are responsible for making sure everything is good and believe they have the power to make everything right. Therefore, they must be responsible for all this sadness. It is hard for women in this situation to allow their parents to manage their own feelings. The baby-loss mom feels pulled to step in and take the pain from her parents.

The pain and sadness of others are not yours to take care of. They aren't yours to manage or to take away. They are not your fault. If you are struggling to recognize the truth, please seek professional counseling. Don't carry these lies any longer. Seeking the truth will be an internal fight. You will battle against years of beliefs, and the truth may remain dim. Find a trusted person to remind you of the truth and to hold on to that new truth.

Although challenging, this may also be a time to develop new boundaries with extended family. Sometimes, although this feels counterintuitive, going to a family event may not be the healthiest choice. You might tell yourself, *If I don't have a valid reason not to go, I have to go.* But maybe allowing yourself an afternoon with friends is better self-care than white-knuckling it through a family barbeque. Or perhaps you can set the boundary of staying only for a limited time. Give yourself permission to do what is best for you.

These boundaries don't mean you will never see your family again. They just mean that on a particular day, you choose self-care rather than falling into old patterns. Today's needs don't define your needs yesterday or next month. Listen to yourself and give yourself what you need. Allow yourself to feel the guilt, recognize that it is invalid—you did nothing wrong to warrant it—and breathe.

Shifting Relationship with God

Your relationship with God can shift as well. Some families lean into God, and though they may not find answers, they find peace and comfort. I have heard from many who have found joy in leaning into God in these times. As Job 1:21 says, "The Lord gave, and the Lord has taken away; blessed be the name of the Lord."

I have also heard from many women and families that struggle to see God as the same loving God from before the death of their child. He blessed them with this child, but then he allowed the child to be taken away. Or worse, it might feel like he took the child away. These families struggle to lean into God.

Many of us learned from an early age that we can trust God. We have felt connected to him and have experienced his love. We learned that he will never fail us. His promises are true. We learned these things in Sunday school, we heard them in church, and we sang about them in songs. Psalm 56:3–4 says,

> When I am afraid,
>> I put my trust in you.
> In God, whose word I praise,
>> in God I trust; I shall not be afraid.

When our child dies, God, at least for a moment, can feel unsafe. We struggle to remember his promises and can struggle to trust and not be afraid. It can feel as if he failed us. We trusted him to keep our child safe, but our child was stolen from us. God can become terrifying because we now know that anyone can die in an instant, including children. It changes the meaning of the platitude "give it up to God."

Trusting God takes on a new reality, and for some, it becomes terrifying. His ways are supposed to be better than ours, but that doesn't feel true at the moment. One woman told me, "It's hard to trust God because I feel like my ways would have been better." It is hard to see how my child dying is better than having them here with me.

For a support person, hearing these laments from a close friend can be sad and scary. It can be hard to hear someone become angry with God and harder still to sit with someone while they verbalize their anger at God. Still, you should allow space for this. Ultimately, we fear that our friend or family member will turn away from God, so we want to push back. We want to defend God and prove that he is still good.

I had a mom and her daughter in my office after they said goodbye to their child and grandchild. While the daughter was trying to tell her mom how angry she was at God and how she didn't like him in that moment, the mom responded with, "You can't feel this way. He didn't do it." She was afraid her daughter would turn her back on God. But God doesn't need us to defend him. God is big enough to hear our anger and to wait for us to come back to him. He will walk with us through this.

Please hear that God is not punishing you. You did not cause your child to die by making him angry. God will love you, regardless of how angry you feel.

Shifting relationships can lead to being closer and more connected, with ourselves and others. Other times we may outgrow the relationship as it is. Remember there is no right or wrong, no should or should not. There is only what works and what doesn't.

Be gentle with yourself in this time of shifting.

QUESTIONS FOR REFLECTION

Do you have a safe person? If so, who?

Do you need to give yourself permission to create a new boundary anywhere? What might that look like?

If you've experienced child loss, have you seen a shift in your relationship with God?

If your friend is the one who experienced the loss, have you seen a difference in how they talk about God?

Chapter 6

THE GIFT OF BEING THERE

Most, if not all, adults have experienced a loss. By a certain age, grieving the death of grandparents is almost guaranteed. We watch our parents pass away. We experience breakups and heartbreak. We have to say goodbye to our beloved pets. And many marriages end in divorce, opening the door to mourning a loss.

We grow up experiencing life as a cycle of loss and healing, often hearing that the experience will make us stronger. How often are we reminded that "What doesn't kill you makes you stronger"? Who hasn't heard "God doesn't give you more than you can handle"? These messages convey that we are to learn from the experience of loss in order to handle subsequent losses.

During these times of loss, we may call upon our friends and family to help; we want someone to bear this pain with us. When a woman experiences a breakup, her girlfriends rally around with ice cream and nights out. Guys gather their buddies and head to a bar for a game of pool and some beer. We need community to rally around us.

When we are faced with losing grandparents or parents, friends often come alongside to help us with our sorrow. Friends offer a shoulder to cry on, a listening ear, and the generous offer to "let me know what you need." Friends take it upon themselves to set up meal trains, send heartfelt texts, and even do our laundry, removing some stress from daily responsibilities. Loved ones rally around us because they genuinely want to help.

All these ways of helping show love and concern. They send the message, "I am here for you." Sometimes they come from a desire to do something when the right words remain elusive.

Are these same actions appropriate after the death of a child? When a child dies or a miscarriage happens, we can be left searching for the best way to help. Yet the trauma of a child's death is much different from a breakup or the death of a parent.

A Senseless Loop

When a child dies, the grieving parents enter a world that no longer makes sense. When a woman delivers her stillborn child, everything she knew to be true is no longer valid. She was just carrying her growing child safe inside her, and then, suddenly, her child is gone. She feels betrayed by her body, the world, and often God. The grieving family begins to search for answers and yet none are found. How do we help in that situation? How do we help someone say goodbye to their child?

According to the National Institute of Child Health and Human Development, in about 25 percent of stillbirths, there is no known reason why the child died.[1] To these parents, nothing makes sense. There is nothing to rally around, nothing to blame, and the world feels like shifting sand.

Parents try to make sense of what doesn't make sense. Their thoughts are on a perpetual loop that plays out over and over. Remember when Alice went down the rabbit hole in the Disney movie *Alice in Wonderland*? She kept falling and falling, finally landing in a world without sense. What she had known to be true no longer fit her experience, and she had to navigate this new world with only her old worldview to guide her. The things Alice knew as absolutes were no longer so. This is the life the grieving family enters.

It is hard to navigate shifting sand alone. Bereaved moms tend to ruminate after a loss. They play out the scenario over and over in their minds, trying to understand it. But there is no sensible thought to grab on to, so they are left in a loop. The brain continues grasping at unformed fragments of thought. We become lost in a daze, trying to develop an unfinished idea into something fully formed.

I want to encourage baby-loss moms whose child died without a diagnosis to recognize the loop. Sit in the senselessness and give yourself freedom to stop looking for the answer. I know how heartbreaking this is to hear, but the answer isn't there. There is nothing you could have done to change the outcome. This was not your fault. I know you have heard this, and I know you doubt its validity, but I will tell you again: this was not your fault.

How can we help someone we love in this situation?

Sometimes the best gift you can offer a grieving parent is the gift of listening, to hear that their world no longer makes sense—without trying to help it make sense. We have to let go of the notion that we have the perfect words to make our friend's situation better. We need to stop believing that we have any words at all. In the time since Abby died, I have learned the immense value of sitting silently with someone while they question the shifting sand. This gesture is a priceless gift.

I know. I hear what I am saying, but there is nothing you can say to help your best friend whose baby just died. I get it. You may want to argue this point. But trust me, there are no words you could tell your friend that will help. That may sound counterintuitive. We are raised to problem solve. If there is an issue, we need to do something to make it better. We aren't often faced with situations that we can't make better.

I know I'm asking a lot. Sitting with someone in their pain, staying present without trying to fix it, is hard. It's frustrating to have no answers.

What bereaved moms want most from you is time to tell you about their child and to mourn. They need time to ponder who their child was supposed to be and to wonder who the child looked like more, mom or dad. They want to lament how unfair this is and question why it happened. Parents often want to verbalize the never-ending loop in their brain because sometimes saying these things out loud quiets the loop, even if just momentarily.

Bereaved moms want to invite friends and family to join them on this journey of grief and to navigate living in the tension of not understanding. If they invite someone in who can't walk with them in this journey, that person becomes unsafe.

These families understand that no one has the answer to the unanswerable. They aren't inviting people to find the answers. They just don't want to be alone. They don't need solutions; they need community.

UNSAFE PEOPLE

After Abby died, my husband and I sought therapy. We weren't desperate for it; I thought it would be a good idea to allow space to process our loss in a therapeutic environment. I had a recurring thought in the back of my brain that marriages break up as a result of traumatic loss, and I didn't want that. (That was me, the therapist, being proactive.) I knew a grief group wouldn't be a good fit for me. I am too much of an introvert, and a group could be overwhelming. So I sought out referrals and found a woman who came highly recommended.

I have no words to describe the experience of visiting the therapist other than *traumatizing*.

As I have mentioned before, I was fragile. My world had shifted, and I was, without being conscious of it, asking someone to know that my world had changed and act accordingly. This was unfair.

Our first session began as I expected. The therapist said, "You two don't seem to be fighting, so what brings you here today?" I looked at my husband, and he answered for us: "Our daughter died." I chimed in, "She was stillborn at thirty-nine weeks." The therapist's response was to ask, "Is that full term? Did she have a name?"

In my brain, without speaking, I exploded with, *Of course she had a name!* I thought that was a stupid question.

In her defense, that may have been her way of asking us what our daughter's name was. Maybe she didn't know what to say and said the first things that came to mind. I don't remember what I said, but I didn't tell her Abby's name at that moment.

I was angry. I felt as if this therapist had just pelted me with two questions that minimized my pain. How could she not know that forty weeks was full term? Although it was unfair, I expected her to know about pregnancy since she was a woman. I don't know if I was upset because of her questions or that Abby had died.

I immediately became defensive and shut down. I no longer wanted to be in this woman's office.

That day, my therapist never asked another question about Abby. Here we were in her office, seeking help to process our loss. I was crying, and I needed her to see my pain. I wanted desperately to talk about Abby. I needed her to ask about my girl.

She became emotionally unsafe. I understand that for many, this would have been a welcome interaction. But I wanted to have a nitty-gritty, in-the-dirt conversation with my therapist. I didn't want to talk about the superficial. Again, this was unfair to her. She had no idea what I wanted, and I didn't have the energy to explain the rupture that occurred. I needed her to see my rawness.

My husband and I attended two more sessions with this therapist. Sessions with her felt like a volleyball game. I wanted to talk about Abby, and she would lobby back asking something about our family history. At some point during our third session, we mentioned that our parents on both sides had children who had died early. My husband lost a sister, and I lost a brother, both before our births.

"Maybe your daughter died," she said without using Abby's name, "so you could understand how your mother felt."

For some, this statement might seem mundane. It didn't impact my husband the way it did me—he chalked it up to being a stupid comment. Those words enraged me. Years later, they still create a pit in my stomach. At the time she made the comment, it didn't sink in completely. I think I was too shocked. We stopped seeing her after that third session. She didn't understand traumatic grief.

I believe we all have unsafe people in our communities. These are people we hold at arm's length, limit our time with, and limit what we share with them. Although we enjoy spending time with them, we are unsure if we can trust them. Sometimes they have been in your life for a long time and you have a shared history. But in the relationship, there has been a shift. The shift may have started gradually or happened in an instant. Too often I have heard that the moment a lifelong friendship shifted and ultimately ended was after a thoughtless comment.

If you're close to a family that has just suffered a stillbirth, chances are that you journeyed with your friends through this pregnancy. You may have been first to know of their joyous news. You helped your friend celebrate her child. You were there through the morning sickness, anxiously waiting to meet the baby. You not only knew how much this child was loved and wanted, but you also loved this child. You became more and more excited, along with your friend, to meet their child face-to-face. But now your friend's baby is gone before they even arrived.

You are grieving not only for your friend but for yourself. Your own grief can often go overlooked. Remember you too have suffered an enormous loss, a death. You are now able to honor your own feelings and sit with your friend in theirs. Few times in life are as gut-wrenching as this. It's time to hear the story of this beloved child who will never grow up. Opening up a conversation, if you and your friend are both in a good moment to do that, is a loving way to be available in grief. Please don't begin a conversation out of obligation or in a moment that doesn't feel right for you. Create dialogue around a new narrative, or lament together.

Here's the thing, sometimes bereaved moms want to talk, and sometimes they don't.

Sometimes the best thing to do is just listen. It is hard to hear a friend or loved one's story of heartbreak, and what could be more heartbreaking than the story of a child dying? It is such a helpless feeling to sit and listen, knowing there is no right thing to say, to see our friend in the most pain a person can bear and realize there is nothing we can do to take that away. But listen to the agony that your bereaved friend is living in.

Sometimes the moment calls for distraction. Bringing food and no expectations can be a lovely gift as well.

If you accept the privilege of walking alongside your friend while grieving what you too have lost, you will be a very safe person indeed.

"Don't Be Sad"

We, as a society, carry a notion that we are supposed to be happy all the time. We think that if we are sad, we are doing life wrong. Unhappiness is a bad thing, and it must be changed. If you are down, then take action; there is no reason why you can't be happy instead. Aren't those the messages we often receive? Think about your own understanding of sadness. In your mind, is it a positive or negative emotion?

In my work with baby-loss moms, I hear many sad stories. Often women seek help because they hear that their sadness is a problem to be solved. In one instance, I was introduced to a woman who came to me after it didn't work out with her previous therapist. She had told him the story of her baby dying within hours of birth. She needed some support. His response to her was, "Don't worry, I will help you get over your grief." She didn't return after that first session. She didn't want to get over her grief; she wanted to carry it. She felt like he was telling her he would help her let go of her baby.

We begin to hear the sad-is-bad message as a child: "Don't be sad." "There is no need to cry." We also receive nonverbal messages that negative emotions aren't allowed. We carry that belief into adulthood and work to avoid feeling anything we deem negative.

And if necessary, there is a pill for that.

Prescribed medication, under the care of a medical doctor, can be a necessary tool for many people. There is no shame in taking medication, nor does the need for medication make us weak. But sometimes allowing ourselves to feel sad, especially when we are grieving, gives us the freedom to experience our humanness. God created us as beings who feel things, including "negative" emotions.

There can be a temptation to self-medicate, although our brains don't use that term. Instead, we think, *This chocolate will make me feel better. Self-medication* is the term used when people turn to devices to relieve pain. We use these things to avoid feeling our emotions. This includes retail therapy; it helps us feel better to buy that new shiny trinket, right? Of course, it's just for three seconds, and then we need the next sparkly thing. Or we justify having a drink with friends to dull the pain by telling ourselves it's social and fun.

There is nothing wrong with shopping or having a drink with friends. In the right context, these things can be excellent self-care. But in the wrong mindset, they can become harmful self-medication.

So when do these behaviors become a concern? When do you know you are self-medicating? If you are using these things to feel numb, or if you become defensive while reading this, then it might be time to look at the behavior more closely. Understandably, we want to numb the pain by any means possible. The challenge comes when we are only numbing our pain. But the more you allow yourself time to sit in the sadness, the less time the grief will continue to feel overwhelming.

The other message society gives us is that if we allow our friends to be sad, we must be failing the friendship. *Maybe I didn't say the right thing. Or perhaps our bond isn't as strong as I thought.* But the strongest relationships are forged in the fire. These are the ones that allow each person to feel the way they need to feel in any given moment, often without speaking. In the silence, the relationship becomes stronger.

I have worked with many women who carry their sadness as a secret. Bereaved parents often say their friends don't want to talk about the loss anymore. The moms perceive that the grief has outstayed its welcome, and it is time to move on, to be the person they were before the pain took over, and to come back to happy. Baby-loss parents are left believing that to maintain the friendship, they must carry this secret. *I have to hide the truth because if my support system knew the truth or how long I have felt depressed, they would leave.* Can you imagine how scary it is to believe that if people knew how sad you were, you would be rejected?

Baby-loss moms want to speak about their child, sometimes for a lifetime. We want our friends to say our baby's name. We want to know that our friends are okay with our sadness.

When we work to take away someone's sadness, we aren't being a true friend. If you are a friend of someone who has experienced baby loss, can you ask yourself the question why? *Why do I shy away from my friend's grief? Is it because it brings up too much sadness in me? Do I feel uncomfortable around someone else's sadness?* I know that feeling sad is never on someone's to-do list for the day. We don't often wake up thinking, *You know, today I want to feel sad.* But why do we work so hard to avoid it? Are we afraid that if we accept our sadness, it will never leave?

Invited to Know the Child

Please hear that having your own experience of grief is okay. One of the most meaningful moments after my daughter died happened while I was still in the hospital. The day after Abby was delivered, my friend came to the hospital, sat on my bed, and cried with me. She walked into the room, we hugged, and we cried. My friend didn't try to make the situation better, and she didn't try to understand what couldn't be understood. I am confident she has no idea how much I value that time with her. I felt as if someone got it. She demonstrated that she understood the amount of pain I was in and that no words could have made it better. That moment solidified her as one of my safest and closest friends.

She met me where I was, and at that moment, she became the face of Jesus.

Maybe your need to avoid their pain isn't fear but rather a belief that it is time for your friend to be done with the grieving process. You've heard that people can get stuck in their grief, and you are concerned this is happening to your friend. Perhaps you fear that the pain will overtake the person, leaving only a shell.

The grief of losing a child will linger for a lifetime. The pain will be something a grieving parent carries with them forever. Just as they would have walked with their child through their lives, the loss of that child will walk with them. This does not mean they are stuck in their grief or that they haven't moved on. This does not mean they are doing life wrong. It just means that their child died.

Can we consider that a lifelong journey of bereavement does not mean someone is stuck in their grief? Can we walk alongside the person and allow time for them to become strong enough to carry the pain and not pathologize them for owning it? As much as bereaved moms don't want to carry this pain, they also want to hold to it tightly. This may be the only part of their child left.

If a child is stillborn, parents don't have memories. Bereaved parents have up to nine months of pregnancy and then the delivery. These parents never got to hear their child laugh or cry. They don't get to experience the firsts of childhood. Bereaved families have only grief to connect them to their child. If the pain goes away, the baby seems to get further and further away. It is a disservice to pathologize someone for holding to the only thing they have of their child.

Can you be the friend who invites conversation about the baby? Can you imagine the gift you could give someone by asking to see pictures or the memory box of their baby? Parents want to share their children with us. Moms desire to hear their child's name spoken by others. We want people to remember our kid's birthdays and to think of them often. What an honor it would be to meet their child.

Isn't it curious that we will talk with a friend about their marriage, breakups and affairs our partners had, financial issues, and other struggles, yet we find it hard to talk about what could be their biggest heartbreak? Is that because we don't have an answer for the unanswerable? Whatever the reason we struggle with these conversations, when we are invited into them, we are being offered an invitation to something precious, and I would never want anyone to miss out on that gift.

Can we find space to listen and hear the pain without needing to answer? Can we be comfortable with someone while they are crying, without the need to make it stop? Can we accept the invitation of listening or offer our own invitation by asking questions?

When you are invited into a friend's story and it becomes challenging to listen, remember to breathe. Take a deep breath. Slow your breathing by counting to three while breathing in. Allow the breathing to calm your emotions, if only for a moment. Breathing allows you a second of reprieve. It will enable you to come back to this moment with your friend and continue to listen.

If, in that moment, you recognize that you are trying to avoid hearing or are working to change the topic, maybe ask yourself why. What do you want to avoid? Give yourself the gift of honesty: If you aren't in your own good place to be with your friend at that moment, that's okay. It is acceptable to say you can't be in that situation right now. That is not a reflection of your friendship. There is no need to push through and be present when you know you can't be.

The sadness from losing a child will, over time, turn into a lifelong journey of grief. If we allow ourselves to witness the strength of a woman carrying this grief, we can be better for it. We will feel emotions more profoundly and experience the world in a new way. We need to be willing to look inward and prepare to be uncomfortable.

Questions for Reflection

What is it like for you to sit in silence?

Do you feel freedom to talk about your child? If not, why not?

If you are friends with a baby-loss mom, do you feel comfortable talking about your friend's child who has died? If not, why not? If so, what are some of the conversations you've had?

Chapter 7

I DON'T WANT TO PRAY

I recently heard a gentleman tell the story of hearing that his daughter had died. He shared that his daughter was attending college away from home, and on a mountain road at night, she was killed in a car accident. This gentleman and his wife had gone to bed believing that their world was safe.

Sometime in the middle of the night, their phone rang. On the other end of the line was someone with the news that their daughter had been tragically killed.

In the next moment, he and his wife quickly got on their knees and cried out to God. They reached for God and leaned in. They experienced a closeness to God that almost can't be defined, such as that mentioned in Philippians 4:7: "The peace of God, which surpasses all understanding, will guard your hearts and your minds in Christ Jesus." They found God amid the heartbreak.

Pastor and author Levi Lusko shared the story of the death of his daughter in his book *Through the Eyes of a Lion*. Lenya, his five-year-old daughter, died while being rushed to the hospital after suffering an asthma attack. It was five days before Christmas. He writes, "Even so, our anchor held. Though we were afraid, we were not alone. . . . We lifted our hands to the air, right there in the ER, and blessed the name of the God who gives and takes away."[1] In the ER, he and his wife held firm to the truth of God.

Levi explains that within moments of his daughter's death, at the urging of his wife, he was able to invite the hospital staff to his church for the Christmas service. He preached at that service five days later. I am in awe that he could do that.

Steven Curtis Chapman, one of my favorite Christian performers, lost his daughter Maria in 2008. She was killed when she was hit by a car in the family driveway. In his book *Between Heaven and the Real World*, Chapman describes the scene in the hospital. While trying to make sense of the sense-less, he and his wife prayed. In that moment of letting their daughter go, they pointed toward heaven. In what was likely the most anguish they will ever experience, they spoke the truth of God to the hospital staff.

Chapman explains, "I had to declare again and again, if for no other reason than to remind myself, 'The Lord gives, and the Lord takes away; blessed be the name of the Lord. God, I'm gonna trust You and Your promises.'"[2]

Other families I have had the privilege of meeting also have lovely testimonies of seeing God in their tragedy. They talk of feeling God's peace throughout the process of delivering and letting go of their child. They share the joy that they experience knowing God is with them.

But what happens when we don't want to pray? What do we do when it is hard to hold on to God's promises? What do we do when we are so angry with God that we don't want to reach for him?

Angry at God

Levi Lusko writes, "I wasn't mad at God, and I never found myself asking or caring why it happened. I was just very angry that it happened."[3]

This is not the story for many.

After a baby dies, the relationship with God often shifts, as I discussed in chapter 5. It might feel like God has changed, but we can be sure that God doesn't change. Hebrews 13:8 says, "Jesus Christ is the same yesterday and today and forever." God remains constant.

As you may remember from earlier chapters, the way we view the world shifts after we lose a child. This impacts our view of God, creating a new experience of God and opening the door to what could be a more profound relationship. As is true with other relationships, many find a deeper relationship with God, but this transformation takes time.

In the weeks after Abby died, I knew I needed God in my healing, but I desperately did not want to talk to him. I wasn't experiencing the peace that surpasses all understanding. I felt great confusion, and I was angry at God. I couldn't understand how he could have allowed this to happen.

I, along with many other families in similar situations, felt abandoned by God. Of course, feeling abandoned by God does not mean God actually abandoned us.

I believe God blessed my husband and me through Abby. She was a gift from God. Yet I struggled to wrap my mind around God giving me the hope of a baby, only to take her away. I struggled to understand Psalm 37:4: "Delight yourself in the LORD, and he will give you the desires of your heart." I was taught that if I was faithful in my asking, then God would answer prayers. I spent nine months believing he had answered my prayer. It is hard to grasp that he gave me the desire of my heart, let me hold it for nine months, allowed me to believe I would have a lifetime, and then took it away.

Many families believe their pregnancy was a blessing, sometimes after years of trying. To have it end in death is hard to fathom. Many women have expressed that it feels cruel. How do we come to terms with the God of love acting cruelly?

Like many women I have talked with, I found myself caught in the middle of knowing that I needed God to continue life but not wanting to lean on him. I have a foundational belief that I cannot navigate life without the guidance of God. I believe he is the one who gives me breath and allows me to wake up each morning, and he either took my daughter or allowed her to be taken from me.

I had, and still have, faith that Abby was made perfect in her death. She is whole and in the presence of Jesus. Baby-loss moms know, without a doubt, that their children don't need them. The challenge is that we want them with us.

Baby-loss moms can struggle with holding on to the promise that God gives the desires of the heart (Psalm 37:4) when they feel he has taken their greatest want. Many women spiral into thoughts of *Did I not desire my child enough? Did I desire my child more than I desired God? Did he take my baby because I sinned?*

After Abby's death, for the first time in my life, I had no desire to be in relationship with God. Let me be clear: I didn't want to turn from God, and I never questioned his presence. I just didn't want to be with him. I was angry and hurt, and I wanted time to heal.

I didn't want to pray, I didn't want people to share with me their experiences of God, and I sure didn't want to hear that he had a hand in what happened. Many women find that they don't feel connected to prayer in the early days after their loss. I don't remember how long this feeling lasted for me, but I have met women who had this experience for days, while others say it lasted for months.

I held on to the promise that God would wait for me. According to Deuteronomy 31:8, "He will be with you; he will not leave you or forsake you. Do not fear or be dismayed." I knew in my gut that he walked beside me, patiently waiting. Some women I have worked with actively avoided God. They said they didn't want him waiting for them and that when they were ready, they would seek him.

Our faith will be stretched and, as a result, can be strengthened. The challenge for baby-loss moms is that trusting God takes great faith. We saw his faithfulness in our pregnancies, we held firm to his blessings, and then everything vanished. To believe that his plan is better than mine is hard when it seems clear that having a baby is a good plan.

This crisis of faith is usually temporary. It can be scary to watch a loved one struggle with this or to listen to their anger. Please allow room for it. It can be terrifying if a loved one appears to have turned from God. Try to remember who this person is and what their heart is like. Give them space for healing. It's not helpful to try to talk someone back into their faith in those moments.

If we work to explain to them God's purpose, we often push them further away. Too many times in our fear that God will be offended, we try to speak our version of God's truth into the situation. But this is not the time to tell your friend that what happened was God's will. These words are not helpful. This creates excruciating pain that is layered on top of existing pain. There is no better way to create an unsafe relationship. I can almost guarantee that nothing will end a conversation faster. More walls will be built up, not only around the friendship but also around the relationship with God. And the baby-loss mom will be left feeling alone, angry, and even more distant from God.

Relationships can become more real and intimate if space is allowed. It may be hard, especially when you want to point your friend toward God. Try to create a nonjudgmental space. Consider why you feel the need to speak into your friend's healing process. Is it because you are afraid or sad? You might try to breathe through what is going on in you. This may not be a good time to ask your friend if they want to pray with you, but you can sit in silent prayer.

If the conversation allows and your motivation is purely to share, then do. If your motivation is to change your friend's perspective, then hold on to your thoughts a little longer. Your job right now is just to listen, not teach. God does not need you speaking for him in this situation.

TRUSTING GOD

Early in my training as a therapist, I learned that it is not uncommon for people to base their perception of God on their earthly father. That was an eye-opening moment. Of course it makes sense that people base their view of God on what they were raised with.

For baby-loss moms, this view can add to the complicated grief process. If their earthly dad was slow to anger and quick to forgive, seeing Father God as full of grace and understanding comes more easily. But imagine if your own earthly dad was hard to trust or became angry easily. Imagine if your earthly dad kept score and held on to wrongs. This would bear weight on your perception of God as trustworthy. Worse yet, imagine if your earthly dad punished you when you became angry or abandoned the family for reasons unknown. Many find having a relationship with God can heal these wounds, but others find it difficult to trust God.

On the other side of loss, depending on our perception, we can think of God as unsafe. He can feel like "yet another" who let us down, and the idea of God's sovereignty can become terrifying. Maybe a better way to describe it is to say we experience the will of God in its limitlessness, and the limitlessness becomes scary. Baby-loss moms have to come to a place where we find trust again.

In Matthew 6:10, Jesus teaches his followers to pray: "Your kingdom come, your will be done, on earth as it is in heaven." This prayer becomes more poignant to a baby-loss mom or a couple that has endured miscarriages. To wholeheartedly pray that we want God's will over our own is where our faith in God confronts our ability to trust him.

Do I have enough faith to allow the reality that God's ways can be different from my own? Can I trust that God will be with me on this path, even if that means letting go of my child?

Proverbs 3:5–6 (NIV) teaches us to

> Trust in the LORD with all your heart
>> and lean not on your own understanding;
> in all your ways submit to him,
>> and he will make your paths straight.

Leaning into God's sovereignty is a scary journey when there is the possibility of experiencing gut-wrenching pain. If we couple that with the trauma of an earthly dad abandoning us, some of us feel terrified to trust God. Can we trust that our heavenly Father is not an earthly dad and, although sometimes painful, his ways are meant for good?

A flood of questions about God can arise in the aftermath of child loss:

> How do I trust God when he allowed my greatest heartbreak?
> We are taught that his will and plan for our lives is much better than our own, yet how can enduring my baby's death be a good plan?
> Isn't it a better plan to let me raise my child on earth?
> Did he allow this because I was going to be a bad mother?
> Was my child going to suffer and he didn't want that?

I know answers to these questions seem like they would provide some comfort. We try to make sense of the senseless by finding these answers. But I encourage you to find the energy to stop asking the questions. I know that can be hard.

We want answers, but I promise that you won't find them, at least not satisfying ones. No one has the answers. This is the tension you will live in—the tension between wanting the answer and knowing there isn't one.

If you struggle to trust God, I encourage you to remember a time when you did have faith, when you saw God's hand in something. Remember a moment when you felt God's closeness or a moment when you knew God loved you. God's ways are good, even when we don't see his goodness. Come back to the promise that God is good, as told in Matthew 5:48: "Your heavenly Father is perfect." We are assured that God is sovereign. He is the great I Am. In Revelation 22:13, we are told, "I am the Alpha and the Omega, the first and the last, the beginning and the end."

Families, especially moms, that experience a crisis of faith want to hold on to the promise that God is good. We want to be able to lean into him. We don't *want* to turn away from the one who is our comfort. We want to go back to when we felt his closeness. But the pain we feel can be too much to allow ourselves time with God. Some women feel betrayed by God.

If leaning into God feels too scary or it is too early to reach toward God, give yourself time. If you have the energy, share these feelings with God. Psalm 62:8 (NIV) exhorts us to "trust in him at all times, you people; pour out your hearts to him, for God is our refuge." He will hear us, and we can trust him. He won't leave.

I know that in the face of losing a child, it is easy to blame him. We think, *He must be at fault. He caused this, and he is being unfair.*

If this is where you are, I encourage you to recognize

where your view of God comes from. If our experiences of our earthly parents dull our view of God, then maybe it is time to recognize the need to forgive our parents. Some people actively hold on to anger as a justification—"This happened to me and I get to be angry about it"—and it creates a barrier to forgiveness. Maybe we need to let go of disappointment from our parents and release ourselves from the anger we are holding on to. Often when we are in a place of recognizing that we are holding on to anger, we come to the end of the road where the anger no longer serves us, and we can then seek forgiveness.

We need to come to a place of accepting that we don't like God's plan and recognizing that it feels unfair, yet trusting him regardless. Just to be clear, God doesn't need this response from us. We need it, because it is healing for us. Holding on to anger and resentment over an extended period can build up. Then those feelings turn to bitterness, and this will linger. Bitterness creates its own set of challenges, including distance from God and continued distrust of people.

People often forgive too quickly. I don't encourage telling yourself that you have moved on from the hurt of your parents without it being true. This happens in relationships all the time. We say "you're forgiven" because we want to go back to happy feelings. But if we come to a place of forgiveness too quickly, it is often not genuine. Our disappointment and anger need their moment too. God is big enough to hear that we don't like what has happened. He is big enough to understand that we are angry and hurt.

Trusting God can feel terrifying because there are many layers to this new recognition of God. This new view is a unique experience of him. We learn to trust God in a new way, knowing that we trust him even when bad things happen. This trust is a submission to his will, regardless of the outcome. It puts into practice the saying, "God is good all the time," which might be nothing more than a platitude coming from someone else's mouth.

Soon after Abby died and we had returned to our church, a woman explained that she had been in a car accident the previous day. She was up in front of the congregation, expressing that God was good because she had not been injured. I am grateful she experienced no injuries. Yet as a baby-loss mom—and I have heard this from others—I thought, *Would you still believe he was good if you had been hurt?*

You see, grieving parents have been in the most heartbreaking places. These parents are confronted with the question, *Do I believe God remains good, even in the most tragic places of my life?* His Scripture declares he does. Can I hold that truth?

Returning to Church

Many baby-loss parents struggle with returning to church since it can create a lot of anxiety. The humanness of the church can feel unsafe for grieving families. They simultaneously anticipate the excitement that church friends will have because of their return and the inevitable sadness caused by words. "Where's your baby?" will inevitably be asked. This question becomes salt in an already gaping wound. How often this question is asked will determine how often the story must be retold.

When people hear the news, they will be shocked, heartbroken, and unsure of what to say. You will hear platitudes, and they could be hurtful. On the other hand, church may be your safe place where you find a lot of healing. If so, soak it in. Cherish the moments you have there.

Friends who have heard what happened will want to come alongside you. Find your safe people, and create whatever boundaries you need. If you want friends to share the news of your loss, great. If you want to be the one to share the news, that is also your choice. If you want to hide out in the bathroom, that works too. Remember that you are navigating new experiences in old territory.

The service may have a different feeling for you as well, and worship can often feel empty. The words could hit a different chord for you, and you might struggle to take them in. You may not believe them. This does not mean you'll never believe them again. Remember that your experience of God is changing. It makes sense that hearing Scripture will feel different as well.

Again, this doesn't mean it will always be that way. Give yourself time and lean into the newness. Recognize what does feel authentic and hold on to those moments.

Prayer could also change. Many families that have experienced this traumatic loss find it difficult to ask for things of God. Talking with God may look much the same, but asking for things changes. Baby-loss families feel powerless in relation to the will of God, so they worry, *Am I asking for something that is not in the will of God? Does my prayer change the will of God? If I pray for healing but healing is outside of God's will, does my prayer change anything?*

The answers to these questions may remain elusive, but we know prayer creates community and relationship with God. When you are ready, talk to God. He will listen. Don't allow your fear or your thoughts to get in the way of a relationship with God.

I encourage you to make a plan for returning to church. Recognize that it is okay if you need to leave early, if you get there and don't leave your car, and even if you walk away from someone in the middle of a conversation. Right now, allow yourself to worry less about what might be perceived, and give yourself the freedom to do what feels right.

At first, church won't feel like it did before your baby died. It may feel the way it used to again in time. For now, find your safe people and create something that feels safe enough.

I hope we can hold on to the truth that God is bigger than any anger we can throw at him. God is the healer; he wants our hurts. And he wants to know our hearts.

Returning to church can be a lonely time for women. Because we are sometimes taught that it is not okay to be angry with God, we often keep these thoughts and feelings buried deep. It feels too shameful to share them, even with our families.

Hold on to what you know to be true. Holding firm to what we know to be true may not feel authentic, but deep inside, you know it is. Hold on to God's promises. Come back to who you know God is; remember the things he has done in the past. If you need help remembering, please ask for help. Find safe people who can help guide you.

If you are in this place of incongruence, please hear that it is okay. You get to be where you need to be. No one gets to tell you that you should be doing things differently. You are not alone.

Questions for Reflection

If you have experienced child loss, did you find yourself angry with God?

Are you able to sit with God? Do you find comfort in him?

If you attended church before your loss, have you returned? If not, why not? If so, what helped you make that decision?

How has your relationship with God changed after moments of great loss or trauma?

Chapter 8

AM I STUCK?

As we have discussed in previous chapters, in the time immediately following a loss, the grief can feel overwhelming. In my work with baby-loss moms, it seems a universal truth that during this period of feeling overwhelmed, they hear this message: Aren't you better yet? This message is either internal, based on previous situations, or from friends. As a result, women begin to feel stuck and wonder if they will ever be normal again.

Because your world is fractured and there is nothing to anchor you, the message that you should be over it can swirl through your mind. This thought is coupled with the fact that the coping skills you used prior to your loss no longer work in this situation. For many, this realm of grief is new territory, unlike anything you have dealt with before.

You may have a strong urge to take to your bed and never leave; I get that. The world just shifted, and your perception of safety was stolen away. What better place to find solace than in your bed? You may find that all you want to do is sleep, or you may not sleep at all. There is nothing abnormal about either of those.

It may take some time to leave the house. Again, this is common. You may or may not want visitors. You may find that you wake up in the morning wanting a friend to come by, and by the time you have had your coffee, you have changed your mind. That's okay.

I worked with a woman who had suffered a late-term miscarriage. She had lost her child at seventeen weeks and believed that because it was "just a miscarriage" she would be back to normal within weeks. She was confused by her inability to follow through with plans she had made. She knew her preloss self well enough that she rarely planned for things in advance, often planning outings for the next day. But now she often woke up on the day of the event only to cancel plans with her friends. Don't feel pressured to keep the date just to make others happy or because that's what you would have done in the past.

Please remember that the journey you are on is not linear. Women I have had the privilege to work with often want to hold firm to the belief that if they feel good enough to leave the house for a walk on Monday, then they have turned the corner and will be *back to normal* by Thursday. These same women are then blindsided when Friday rolls around and they don't want to get out of bed. On this nonlinear journey, you will have moments that flip between being devastated and feeling less sad, peppered with moments that feel good.

There will come a day when you feel frustrated because you anticipated feeling good. You will have a solid run of four days that feel almost back to the way life used to be, and then on the fifth day you will wake up in a pit of sorrow. This does not mean you are stuck. This does not mean you have gone backward in your healing.

If you still find it difficult to leave your bed or the house after a few weeks, then reach out for help. Staying in bed during a grief-filled day is typical. But staying in bed and sleeping the days away could be a sign of depression. Not all grieving moms are depressed, and I don't want to suggest that a day in bed is a sign of depression. I would suggest reaching out for help if you spend more days in bed than out, if you find it difficult to stay awake more days than not, or if you find that your appetite has changed.

Baby-loss moms begin to wonder if the pain will ever go away. We question how the pain could ever subside. Many wonder how to live life with the grief of losing a child. The immediate aftermath of loss is not the time to plan the future or look ahead to imagine life without this pain. In this place, focus on only now, breathing in and out. Staying in the present may take effort. You might have to remind yourself to stay there. Sometimes this means speaking out loud (when alone) or sometimes quietly in your head. Remember the rubber-band trick from chapter 4? If you find it hard to keep your thoughts in the present, snap the rubber band. In conjunction with snapping the rubber band, shift your attention to something around you. Bring your thoughts back to the present.

Many believe it would be easier never to wake up again than to live with the pain. It is normal to have that thought; this is not necessarily an indication of being suicidal. It is a giant leap from not wanting to wake up to wanting to die. After burying their child, many women just don't care if they live or die. They find it hard to care about anything. Again, it is a giant leap from not caring if you live or die to wanting to die.

Many moms believe they would rather be with their dead child than face life without them. If you find that you do want to die or harm yourself in any way, please seek professional help. Call the suicide prevention hotline. Reach out. There are good therapists and counselors out there who understand. They will walk alongside you in the loss without trying to take your grief from you.

Hearing that a loved one doesn't want to wake up can be terrifying. It sounds as if they want to die. It will be challenging to not react to this, but I encourage you to listen. This is a natural response to traumatic grief. Recognize your own fear, and notice if your response to your friend is out of that fear. Some signs are cause for concern, and I would encourage seeking help. These include your loved one sharing with you a plan for how they will die, more than once they express that they are a burden to you, they start giving away their possessions, their use of alcohol increases, and they begin to withdraw. This is not a definitive list, and I encourage you to seek help if you feel the need, even if the only purpose of seeking help is to alleviate your own fears.

This isn't the time for tough love or to give someone a pep talk. As I've mentioned a few times now, this is a time just to sit back and listen. Remember, you are also grieving the relationship that was and navigating a new relationship that now includes grief.

INTEGRATING YOUR GRIEF

Grief can walk hand in hand with happiness. It seems that many people carry a misconception that if they feel happy, they can't be sad at the same time. A great example of this is when change occurs. Have you ever felt a little sad when you were promoted? Or when you purchased a new car? We sometimes experience a little grief of loss when we are given new opportunities. We are complex beings, and we can carry more than one emotion at a time. This seems never to be more true for a baby-loss mom than during the holidays. The sadness over the loss of our child is intermingled with the joy of seeing Christmas through our living children's eyes.

We forget, or were never taught, that we are strong enough to carry the pain. We are strong enough to experience joy while carrying pain. We are strong enough to carry the weight of the memory of our children. We can come to a new experience of life where grief and joy coexist. It is a life in which grief is respected for what it is and isn't defined as wrong.

When you forget that truth, just breathe. Don't look for answers; don't look for meaning; just breathe.

Yes, you will feel extraordinarily sad. You will cry and wonder when the crying will stop. You will miss your baby and have many unanswerable questions. You may wonder about the future and if the future holds any more babies for you. These responses are all common. Please allow yourself a moment to stop looking for answers. You will stop crying at some point.

Remember, breathe in and breathe out.

You will come to a day when you don't have to remind yourself to breathe. You will come to a day when breathing feels less painful than it did the day before. Hold on to those moments. The more you can do so, the more they will connect together and build into longer periods. Then one day you'll recognize that you no longer have to remind yourself to breathe at all.

Childcare

It can be challenging to navigate this new world that includes grief while caring for children in the home. Depending on their ages, they may need hands-on care. When getting out of bed is difficult, feeding our children creates a whirlwind of emotions and struggles. How do I feed my child when I don't care if I ever eat again?

Please allow yourself to rely on others. This is an excellent time for friends to step in. What a gift to let friends care for your family. If you have enough emotional energy, there might be an inclination of guilt. Recognize your inability to fill the need, there is no guilt in that. You are taking care of your family.

In the newness of integrating grief, some baby-loss moms find they need to give themselves permission to feel okay. This does not mean the grief is gone; it is making a home inside you. It becomes part of your internal world, informing your worldview.

Some baby-loss moms feel the need to hold tight to the initial sting of the pain. This is where they feel closest to their child and still get to hold them. It is a sacred place. Allowing yourself time and movement away from that sacred place does not mean you leave your child there. Your baby, just like the grief, finds their space in whatever home you put them in. They stay with you. This becomes the new sacred place that is shared only by you and your baby.

As with most baby-loss moms, I remember the first time I caught myself laughing after Abby died. I stopped myself mid-laugh. I wondered if it was okay to laugh, or maybe I was surprised that I did laugh. How could I find anything funny after losing my daughter? I took a second, and then I reminded myself that my laughing wouldn't take away Abby's memory. It also didn't mean I missed her any less. Abby still has her place, and if she were here, she would laugh too. (And, yes, I wish I could have heard her laugh.)

TIME TO MOVE ON?

In the aftermath of loss, as time continues, you will experience a shift in how others interact with you. Conversations change, and you may wonder if others have forgotten what happened. This shift happens gradually and often goes unnoticed until it feels like a smack in the face.

Is It Getting Better?

You will begin to see a difference in the questions from others. Fewer people will ask, "How can I help?" And more will ask, "Is it getting better?" It is important to note that the intent of these questions is never to be hurtful or dismissive. The purpose is still to show care and concern for a loved one. It can be another form of asking how to help. But the implication is that it is time to move on.

For baby-loss moms, this question is a dagger in the heart. When I was first asked, "Is it getting better?" soon after Abby died, I wanted to scream, "How can you ask me that? It will never be better!" I believed that I would never be okay again.

I, like many others, thought that to be okay, I had to let go of my grief.

The question, "Is it getting better?" feels like a setup. It has only two answers: yes or no. If I respond with a yes but inside still feel the full weight of grief, then I don't feel safe to answer honestly. I might believe the lie that I should feel better by now. This can create a distance in friendship while perpetuating fear. I might wonder, *Do I have to fake it?* Faking it is exhausting.

If I answer no, then am I stuck? What if after six months the answer is still no? What is the appropriate time frame in which to get better? Is that timeline determined by me or by society? And what does being "better" even mean?

Here is the challenge: people base their thoughts on the assumption that grief has a time limit, and I want to challenge that. Traumatic grief has no time limit. There is no right or wrong way. Most importantly, no one gets to tell you how to grieve.

Closure and Meaning

Some suggest that baby-loss families can get stuck in grief. I have even heard it suggested that women choose to stay stuck, especially in the case of miscarriage. I respectfully disagree. I suggest that in the circumstance of burying a child or suffering a miscarriage, getting stuck in grief should not be considered as a possibility. Baby-loss moms make a choice to hold on to the memory of their child, and that goes hand in hand with grief.

One father who tragically lost his daughter told me he will never let the grief go. He holds on to it because that is his connection to his daughter. A friend or outsider's job isn't to take that away or tell him he is grieving incorrectly. Their job is to walk alongside him on his journey.

I have heard it said that to move on, closure is necessary. Some grief experts will tell you that to find healing you must find meaning. But here's the deal: Closure is not real. It is a myth.

I want to challenge this thinking. It could be impossible to find meaning in the death of your child. Enduring multiple miscarriages doesn't make sense, and anyone would be hard-pressed to find meaning in it. I certainly don't believe that those who don't find meaning or closure are stuck.

Sometimes meaning can't be found. And where one person finds meaning, another person won't. Some women find that their loss can help so many others; other bereaved moms are offended at the notion of their loss being used to help others. These women don't find meaning in that.

Friends may want to help by attaching meaning that isn't welcome. They say things like, "I now know what signs of trouble to look for in my pregnancy because of your experience." Yet it is no consolation to a baby-loss mom when your pregnancy goes much smoother as a result of her child's death.

If meaning can't be found, that does not mean you are stuck. It also doesn't mean you aren't healing correctly. It is okay if, over time, no closure comes.

Talking about Your Child

Another misconception is that women who choose to talk about their child are somehow stuck. If she says her baby's name, she must not be over their death. Women who choose to talk about their baby or miscarriage are not stuck. The issue is with the person who finds discomfort in hearing the baby's name. Women who bury their child need the freedom to say their child's name. Women who have suffered miscarriage need to be given the freedom to speak of their experience. This is one way women can honor their children.

STUCK IN FEAR AND GUILT

One place women *can* get stuck is in the fear of the what-ifs. It presents as guilt. Isn't guilt just hiding our fear that we did something or didn't do something that caused pain?

I have not met one woman who has said goodbye to their child who hasn't struggled with guilt. I also have never met a woman whose guilt about the death of her child was valid. I bet if you asked a baby-loss mom about her guilt, she could point to the moment when she believes she should have done something different.

My moment was the Friday before delivering Abby. It was after my doctor's appointment, and Abby did what felt like a flip in my stomach that was bigger than any I had experienced. It felt as if she stretched out all her limbs at once and did a backflip. I was talking to my husband and stopped midsentence to comment on it. I hold on to that moment as one in which I should have known there was a problem and done something. In moments of fear, I wonder if this was the moment that Abby suffered. Did I let my baby die? If I allow it, this story can loop in my mind: *A well-attuned mother would have known something was wrong. I must not be a good mom because I missed something so terrible that it killed my daughter.*

Here is the truth: I don't know what happened with Abby.

We don't know why she died. There were no conclusive tests that pointed to a reason. I don't have the right to hold on to something that isn't true as the reason my daughter is not here.

My only hope is to recognize the lie as fear and release it.

Other women have similar stories about moments in their pregnancies they wish had been different or times when they wish they had acted differently. Some moms hold on to that part of the story as truth without any proof. It becomes an answer to what is unanswerable, a way to make sense of why their baby died.

Holding on to these lies as truths keeps us stuck in a merry-go-round of guilt and fear. Recognizing our fear allows freedom.

The challenge is this: We are fearful because we have little power. We have no control over our pregnancies. We can do everything right and still have to let go of the outcome. This is a terrifying truth for women who have said goodbye to their children.

We want to do anything to avoid feeling this fear. We will stay on that merry-go-round for all eternity to prevent feeling powerless over the protection of our unborn children. Please don't hold this fear alone. Speak about it. Journal about it. These things can help you release it.

Could there come a time when seeking professional help could be useful? Absolutely. Is it always necessary? Probably not. Would it be a bad idea? No, it never is. If you are experiencing a never-ending loop of the what-ifs, then reach out. If your anxiety keeps you awake or interferes with life, then please seek help. Find a good therapist or counselor to walk with you on this journey.

THE FIRST YEAR

The first year is the one with the most anticipatory weariness. It feels heavy. Not only does the pain feel the most intense, but you become acclimated to life with grief. Within the first year, baby-loss families are confronted with all the firsts: the first month without their child, the first Easter, the first Christmas. These firsts are hard and can feel overwhelmingly sad.

This is normal. You said goodbye not only to your baby but also to who they were going to be. The family you dreamed of is gone. This loss is highlighted in the first year without them.

In the first year, baby-loss moms experience all the should-bes. They begin in the hospital with thoughts like, *I should be breastfeeding or learning to breastfeed my baby. I should be bathing my baby.* These thoughts take up a lot of space in a new mom's mind in the first year.

These should-bes are the idealized version of motherhood. The mom has no other choice because there is no baby with whom to live out reality. So the mom lives in a dream world of daily check-ins of what her baby should be doing. *My baby should be walking. My baby should be laughing.*

When these thoughts are verbalized to loving friends and family, they are often met with the answer, "You can't think that way." Telling someone not to think a certain way only causes that person to think that way more. This could be a great moment to allow a mom to process their continued grief through what *should be* rather than what *is*. What is often thought of as a pity party or wallowing is actually a form of processing.

This conversation could be uncomfortable. If you are a friend who has told a baby-loss mom to stop thinking about the milestones, recognize what is going on in you. Allow your own discomfort, and acknowledge that living through this first year is much harder for your friend than for you.

The first year is punctuated by firsts that only remind baby-loss parents that the baby isn't here. That reality is so unfair. You may find yourself in moments of new feelings that you don't expect. You might find yourself crying one day out of the blue. This is fine. Please don't hold on to the lie that the crying should stop after a few months. You are not stuck in your grief. It's okay to miss your baby.

The holiday season, beginning with Halloween, is often the hardest time of that first year for parents. It can bring the biggest disappointment. Parents who have said goodbye to their child because of stillbirth have dreamed of their baby's first Halloween costume. They've imagined family members meeting their child for Thanksgiving dinner. They anticipated the first family Christmas card. But they don't get to experience the joy of those traditions and celebrations with their child.

Families can find some comfort in creating room for their child. For some, this means buying a new outfit you wish your child could have worn. Others find Christmas stockings to hang or an ornament for their baby. Many have family pictures taken with a stand-in for their child, such as a teddy bear or pair of shoes bought for their baby.

The first holidays can also raise a more significant awareness that others around you have children. You may question whether to spend time with relatives with children. You might question whether you participate in extended family holidays at all. That is a valid question. You have the choice to honor yourself in any way that you need to around the first holidays.

If the choice is made to skip tradition and create a new experience that year, remember again that this does not mean you are stuck in your grief. It does not mean you aren't healing from your loss. It is okay to take care of you the way that feels the most peaceful.

The first birthday can also be very painful. It can bring about a time to reflect on the things you missed: the first steps, the laughing, and more. It will bring about more questions of what your child would be like. Many baby-loss families have birthday parties; others choose not to have a party. Either option is great if that is your choice.

I have heard too many times that having a party feels weird. (Often people mean that it would be perceived as strange.) No, it is not weird to have a Disney-themed party because you believe your daughter would have loved it. It is a lovely way to honor your baby. You aren't responsible for anyone else or their thoughts.

Families find comfort in remembering or celebrating their child once a year. On October 25, 1988, President Reagan designated October as Pregnancy and Infant Loss Awareness Month. His proclamation states,

> Each year, approximately a million pregnancies in the United States end in miscarriage, stillbirth, or the death of the newborn child. National observance of Pregnancy and Infant Loss Awareness Month, 1988, offers us the opportunity to increase our understanding of the great tragedy involved in the deaths of unborn and newborn babies. It also enables us to consider how, as individuals and communities, we can meet the needs of bereaved

parents and family members and work to prevent causes of these problems. . . .

Now, Therefore, I, Ronald Reagan, President of the United States of America, do hereby proclaim the month of October 1988 as Pregnancy and Infant Loss Awareness Month. I call upon the people of the United States to observe this month with appropriate programs, ceremonies, and activities.[1]

On or around the middle of October every year, baby-loss moms and families carry an extra heaviness. They may feel more emotional or cry without provocation. October is another reminder of what we miss.

There will never be a season when your child leaves your mind. You may not think about your child every minute, but the thoughts will always come. Carrying the grief of your child for a lifetime does not mean you are stuck in your grief. It means you are an amazingly strong person carrying a pain the size of your child.

QUESTIONS FOR REFLECTION

After experiencing child loss, did you want to stay in bed? What helped you get out?

Do you remember the first time you laughed after your loss? What was that experience like for you?

What do you want people to know about you and your loss? (If you are friends with someone who experienced loss, ask them this question.)

Chapter 9

"HOW MANY KIDS?"

O ne day someone will ask, "How many kids do you have?" This may be the thing you fear most: meeting new people and innocent conversation. These words will make you suck in your breath. This seemingly simple question becomes terribly complicated when you have buried your child.

I have never had a baby-loss parent tell me there is an easy answer to this question. The parent always wants to give an answer that includes all the kids, both living and not living. This can create an uncomfortable situation.

Here's the thought process: *If my answer includes my unliving child, then I am left with the possibility of having to manage the other person's response. But if I answer without adding my unliving child, then am I honoring my baby? This is my child and should be part of the answer.* This is a valid struggle for a baby-loss parent.

In response to the "how many kids" question, I encourage parents to answer in whatever way feels right in the moment. Please don't feel pressure to be untrue to yourself and what feels right. Remember, you don't need to take care of someone else and their reaction. Don't let someone's discomfort—or more often than not, *fear* of their discomfort—make you answer in a way that doesn't feel true and honest.

This will become your new normal: wishing that an innocent question could have a simple answer, that you didn't feel confusion around holidays, and that seeing a stranger's child didn't leave you wanting to cry for no apparent reason. Part of the confusion with this new normal is that parents are left feeling "off." This feeling can happen at any point during any given day and usually catches us off guard: we get triggered.

TRIGGERS

We all have triggers, and they can be tricky. We may know what our triggers are; we may not. A particular smell can trigger us. The direction of the wind can trigger us. It is impossible to avoid all triggers, so we manage them. We give ourselves grace when we feel fragile. We make space.

Being human means we can feel more than one emotion at the same time. We have space to be happy and sad at once, and both feelings can be true for us at any given moment. Or you might find yourself feeling sad in the morning, happy moments later, and sad again after that. This does not make you crazy. This is the privilege of being human.

You may find yourself on the verge of tears for no discernable reason. That's okay; you don't need to go looking for their cause. Give yourself time to lean into the tears. Crying is not a sign of weakness. It takes courage to feel the sadness. If you find one day that you are extra angry for no apparent reason, that's fine too. Be okay with taking a moment to be in the anger.

Pregnant Women

Seeing a pregnant woman can be a trigger. It's as if you have a homing beacon attracting all the pregnant women around you, and you can't get away from them. You see them everywhere. Child-loss mothers often tell me how much they hate these pregnant women. This is normal. This can cause guilt in the baby-loss mom because we are taught as children that *hate* is a bad word. But in this case, the "hatred" comes out of sadness. Underneath everything, it's usually the situation, not the pregnant woman, that is despised. Give yourself grace in this.

If you are the friend of a baby-loss mom, this isn't the time to tell her, "You don't really feel that way." Nothing is more aggravating to a baby-loss mother than to hear from someone else how she is feeling or what she should be feeling. Instead, acknowledge how sad it must be to see a woman experiencing what your friend should be experiencing. Remember who your friend is: probably not someone filled with hate.

Other Children

I wish it weren't the case, but other people's children can trigger pain. Baby showers are painful. Birthday parties are unpleasant. Give yourself permission to do what feels right in any given situation. Today might not be a great day to attend a baby shower, but tomorrow could feel right to go to a child's birthday party. Be flexible. Be aware of what you need.

It is not uncommon for women who have just lost a child or suffered a miscarriage to delay meeting a friend's new baby.

There is no harm in giving yourself some time. I have worked with many women who have taken months before they felt ready to see their friend's new baby. It takes a lot of courage to take that step and even more courage to hold their friend's child. Again, I know this is unfair. You want to celebrate the new baby and to love them. Give yourself time.

Please don't rush into seeing a baby too soon. This isn't a time to push yourself into "what should be." It is common to feel jealous of what your friend has. Hold on to the understanding that this feeling will dissipate over time. It is part of the journey. Allow space to be fully present when you can.

The Due Date

Women who have suffered a miscarriage can begin to feel the due date's weight. This can come out of the blue, or it may loom. Some women wake up on that day, unaware of its significance, only to be reminded midway through.

Other women live through what would have been nine months of pregnancy asking things like, *How big would my baby be now? I should be feeling my baby kick or move.* As the weight of the due date becomes more prominent, a new sadness emerges. All the should-haves come into play. *I should have had a shower. I should have had a babymoon. I should be arranging a nursery and a diaper bag.*

There is no best way to acknowledge the due date, but please do so in some way. You could have friends help you recognize it. You could choose to mark it with a day at your favorite place. You can choose to acknowledge it for a moment and then release it. Please don't try to forget or ignore it. Honor your baby and your feelings by being aware of it.

Many friends won't remember the date. If you are the friend of someone who miscarried and you do know the date, please don't let it pass without acknowledging it. Reach out. This will not cause any unnecessary sadness; you will not bring up something your friend forgot or doesn't want to talk about. Please bring it into the open.

Mother's Day

Mother's Day can be a beast. Right around April, when you are inundated with emails and commercials about Mother's Day, you may begin to feel a heaviness. You may think, *I was supposed to celebrate motherhood on this day. How do I do that when my child died? How do I hold firm to my identity as a mother if my only child isn't with me?* Many baby-loss mothers stop watching TV to avoid these commercials. Then right after Mother's Day, before you can catch your breath, it's Father's Day. These days can be painful and hard to navigate.

"Rejoice in hope, be patient in tribulation, be constant in prayer," Paul writes in Romans 12:12. Please allow yourself some patience, and be gracious with yourself. You may find you're tired for no reason, feel off, or unaware that the effects of the holiday are lingering. There's a reason you feel short-tempered. Again, this is normal.

Mother's Day and Father's Day hold an inherent challenge: other people celebrate them. You might be faced with how to manage honoring your own parents on these holidays. Give yourself permission to do what you need to do. It might feel right for you to stay home that day or find a peaceful place to sit and reflect. You may want to be alone with your spouse.

You may want to be surrounded by family. Either option is excellent, as long as it feels calming for you.

If you are a parent of someone who experienced a stillbirth or miscarriage, please recognize the pain these days can bring to your child. If they need to not celebrate, try not to take it personally. This could be true some years and not true others. Their hesitation is not about your relationship, but rather their inability to be present. Almost all baby-loss moms wish they could compartmentalize their grief for the sake of their own mothers.

For baby-loss parents who have a living child, these holidays can carry a particular weight. The child celebrates their parents, which is lovely, but the parents miss their nonliving child, which is painful. Baby-loss moms describe Mother's Day as special yet can feel really sad. They try not to minimize the celebration and try to stay present to enjoy it, but this effort can be draining.

The First Birthday

Then the baby's first birthday begins to loom. When your child's first birthday comes around, it is okay to celebrate it. I know many families that throw a birthday party for their child. Plan it any way you want. Invite whomever you want to. Buy an amazing cake, balloons, and birthday hats. Celebrate your child. There is nothing abnormal about having a birthday party to tell the world that your child existed.

If you want friends to bring gifts, then ask them to. You can donate the items, give them to other people's kids, or hang on to them. There is no wrong way to celebrate. Too many families don't have parties because they hear people say it's "weird." If you want to celebrate or remember, please don't let anyone take this experience away from you.

But if you don't want to throw a birthday party, that's okay too. I will warn you that trying to do normal life on your child's birthday is difficult. You may prefer to shut yourself away from the world because you want to be quiet. Please feel the freedom to take care of yourself on this day.

I have also learned that birthdays feel different each year. Some birthdays come and the grief feels extraordinarily heavy. In those years, the longing for our kids seems to linger. On the other hand, some birthdays come with just a flicker of longing. Each year brings with it a vision of who our child would or should have been. For many parents, this is a great time to write a letter to their child, sharing life with them and the dreams they wanted for their child.

The First and Last Day of School

As the summer comes to a close and the first day of school shows up, sadness can come along with it. Parents are reminded that their child isn't there to walk to school. They are left to wonder who their kids would have been during this stage in life. What would they be like as students? What would their favorite subject be? The same is true for the ending of the school year. We seem to feel the heaviness of what our kids missed.

While I was pregnant, I told people that I wanted to buy Abby a pair of red Vans shoes. I still envision her walking to school wearing those red shoes.

Many women feel a weight lift with the passing of the first year. The day after the birthday, you may look back and realize you survived the year. Yes, you did. While triggers will still be out there, you can hold on to the truth that you are a strong woman who lived through the first year after her child died.

THE NEXT PREGNANCY AND RAINBOW BABIES

Deciding to try for a subsequent pregnancy after a loss can carry anxiety. Be sure to get your doctor's clearance before trying. Many families want to wait for the right time, but finding that perfect time is difficult. It may never feel right. Some couples find it helpful to stick to the original plan for the timing of children. This plan can take the weight of your feelings out of the decision.

Please be aware of any anxiety you may feel. Many friends will want to support you in the decision to "try again." They will want to come alongside you with supportive words and actions. May I be direct for a moment? If you are one of these friends, please don't say, "It won't happen again," "It never happens twice," or "What are the odds it would happen again?"

The truth is that it can and does happen again to many families. Don't try to uplift your friend with what could be a lie; whatever the true percentage is, baby loss can and sometimes does happen to a woman more than once. Saying it can't happen again won't be comforting. Baby-loss moms know in their gut that it can.

Women who have suffered a stillbirth don't have faith in the odds. When their child died, they heard the statistics were low. When Abby died, a doctor came into my hospital room and said there was less than a 1 percent chance for this to have happened. Well, guess what, it did. Statistics mean very little when your child dies.

If you are a friend, don't use statistics to try to help. Be supportive through listening and celebrating when a subsequent pregnancy happens. Listen to your friend's fears and anxiety. Allow room for the unknown.

If you become pregnant after loss, remind yourself that history does not determine the present. This is a new pregnancy. All pregnancies are different, even if they feel the same. Please try not to look for similarities between your pregnancies; these similarities don't mean you'll have the same outcome.

Plan with your doctor how you will manage your fears during this pregnancy. Remember that your anxiety could be heightened, and allow for that. Stay focused on the present, not the past or the future.

Delivering a "rainbow baby"—a healthy baby after loss—is a joyous occasion. You may have a flood of emotions, ranging from pure joy to relief. But this experience can also come with guilt and sadness. Women often struggle with those feelings and, as a result, hide them. The voice in your brain might sound something like this:

I just lived through a terrifying experience. History taught me not to expect a happy ending, but now I got one! Phew.

I am reveling in the love I have for my child. They appear perfect, and I am filled with indescribable tenderness.

I miss my baby. I am staring into the eyes of my newborn child, wondering what my previous child's eyes would have looked like.

These thoughts are common but, for many moms, unexpected. Many parents don't anticipate feeling anything but joy at the birth of their rainbow baby. It is normal to look into the eyes of what you longed for, missing what you had to give up.

The hospital itself may trigger the feelings you had the last time you delivered. The experience of birth, the smells, and the energy in the room can activate unwanted emotions. They may linger under all the excitement and activity of the new birth experience; it is crucial to be aware of them. You may choose not to heed them at that moment, and that's okay. Feel the freedom not to engage with those feelings now. But when the time feels right, I encourage you to allow a moment with those feelings.

Many families find that using the furniture that was bought for the baby that died is practical, but it brings up challenges as well. They think that because the furniture was never used, there should be no issue. Sometimes that is true; sometimes it's not. Using the hand-me-down furniture is yet one more reminder that your baby died. The baby didn't need this furniture. Hand-me-down clothes and toys bring up the same thoughts. Seeing your new child enjoying what was supposed to be your first child's can cause a stirring. For some, it brings anger, for others, guilt.

Repurposing the crib may not be the right choice. If you find that you want to cry every time you see it or find it challenging to stay in the present, you may determine a new crib is necessary. Depending on many factors, including the intensity of the emotions, the practicality of repurposing furniture may not warrant using it for a second child.

STILL MOTHERS

There is a term for mothers who never have another child: a still mother. Many wonder, *Am I still a mom?* The answer is yes. You are forever a mom.

This is not the journey you thought you would be on, and for most of you it is not the road you wanted. This is not the label you asked for or the group you wanted to be in. I am sorry this is the path you are on. I wish it were different for you.

Loved ones often offer advice in this situation, usually unsolicited. The one I hear most is "You should adopt." Adoption is an excellent option if that is what you choose. But if you are a friend of a still mom, please just listen. Advice about infertility treatments, adoption, or what you would do is often unhelpful. We know those words are said with good intentions and that you just want to see your friend happy. But the message received is that we aren't complete until we have a child. That implication carries a lot of pressure and isn't true.

If your story does not include a living child, please hear that you are enough. Raising a child here on earth does not define you. You are still you.

Part of being human is wanting what we don't have. Some of us get only a taste of what we want, like a pregnancy without the joy of raising our child. Others have dreams that aren't made a reality, longing for a child but suffering infertility or multiple miscarriages. The whys—*Why didn't I get this? Why did that person get it, but not me?*—can feel unfair. These are the questions that, if allowed, can swallow you whole.

Carrying the grief of our children is part of our story, one in which God walks alongside us. The goal is to accept what is given to us and find moments of gratitude along the way. I hope there are moments in which you even find joy, even when you wish those moments could be different.

In my baby-loss journey, accepting that a living child is not part of my story carries another level of loss. It means letting go of a dream in order to be okay with what I have. This process can create an opportunity to find new hope, even in the despair of letting go of what I wanted. Give yourself time to grieve the dream.

Memorials, Rituals, and Remembering

Many families find comfort in honoring their child, whether or not they have other children, through memorials and rituals.

In the early stages of grief, memorial services and funerals are common. A memorial service allows family and friends to join us in our grieving, engaging us in community. Friends and family rally around us by setting up meal trains, dropping off flowers, and delivering gift cards.

As time passes, though, rituals will become more intimate. You may decide to visit the burial site at regular intervals, finding connection to your child there. Many parents partake in the ritual of saying goodnight to their child every day and kissing their child's picture. Families plant trees, build monuments, or find a connection to their child through nature.

Many parents write letters to their children on their birthdays. Others write poetry or find connection through art. It is not uncommon for a parent to get a tattoo honoring their child, even parents that would never get a tattoo under other circumstances. It is a tangible representation of carrying their child with them wherever they go. It can also be a conversation starter, allowing the parent to share the story of their child. As time passes, families may participate in fundraising walks to raise awareness, candle-lighting vigils, or community memorials.

Those who have suffered miscarriage may find peace in honoring their lost ones as well. There is no right way to honor your child when a miscarriage happens. Find something that brings peace. If you feel led, have a service, plant a tree, or create a scholarship fund. Create a yearly ritual that will become part of your family activities, or hold a one-time remembrance. Whatever feels right to you.

If you are a friend of someone who has experienced child loss, how can you help? Reach out on important dates, birthdays, holidays, and the anniversary of the loss. It is touching to have a friend remember your child's birthday. If you're so inclined, bake a cake or bring flowers. Donate to a worthy cause in the child's name. Don't let the anniversary go by without reaching out.

Say the baby's name. We want our child to be part of the conversation. Dream about the child with your friend. Imagine who that child would have been and what they would have been like. Families want their child to be remembered. They want their child to be recognized as a person who existed.

I've had the privilege of working with a baby-loss mom after her first daughter was stillborn at thirty-seven weeks. She wrote the following:

> I think the most important thing I want people to know is that to know the real me, you have to know the "me" with my daughter. She will always be a part of my life and has forever changed who I am. I am on a life long journey of discovering who she is, learning more about her, and

myself through the process. If you don't allow that to happen, or cannot meet me in that space, you can never know the full, real me. Asking about her, saying her name, and telling me you think of her are just some of the ways people have shown me that they want to enter into life with my daughter and me. Of course, their experience of life with my daughter is different from mine. I am her mom, and every day I live with the reality that she is not physically here and all of the ramifications of that. Even though some are willing to, as messy and hard and even uncomfortable as it is at times, it brings me joy and peace to know she is continuing to impact others.

QUESTIONS FOR REFLECTION

If you've experienced child loss, what is your response when asked how many children you have?

Do you have a memorial for your child? If so, what is it?

Do you celebrate your child's birthday? If not, why not? If so, how?

Have you experienced subsequent pregnancies? If so, what were they like for you?

Chapter 10

MY HUSBAND'S STORY

I met my husband, Shadrach, while we worked together in the mid-1990s. Before my life as a therapist, I worked in the accounting field. He and I met while we worked at a university in town, about ten years before we married. I worked in the business department, and he was the shy, quiet guy across the hall in the IT department.

Shadrach was the guy I would call when I needed help with my computer and when my printer stopped working. He jokes that he had to be nice to me because I was the one who did payroll. Shadrach has the biggest heart and always wants the best for people. He is kind and will drop everything to help others, always seeing the best in others. This is one of the things I love most about my husband, and I loved it about him even before he was my husband.

He and I were part of a group of friends that sometimes hung out after work. We often ate lunch together, and we would make weekly ice cream runs while we were supposed to be working. I remember those days fondly.

NIKKI

During those days, I was married to my first husband, and soon after Shadrach left the school, he met the woman he would marry. Her name was Nichole, but everyone called her Nikki. I heard about her one night after work while he and I were waiting for other friends to show up. I was struck by how much he seemed to like her. He explained how great she was, and I got to hear his plans for their first date. He looked happy, and I was excited for him.

It's fun to tell the story of when I went with Shadrach to pick up Nikki's engagement ring. He was so happy and had no doubt that he was making the best decision of his life. He presented himself so differently from a year earlier; he had become confident and sure of himself. I was happy that he had found someone to love. That is part of our story, part of our history together. I get to tell friends that I helped him find his first wife's wedding ring.

On one of the hottest days in the middle of the summer, I was blessed to attend their wedding. By that time, I had left the university as well. Shadrach continued building his career in the computer world, and I began a master's degree in psychology. We soon lost touch. Shadrach started a new married life, and I tried to stay afloat while my marriage continued to unravel. Soon I endured a painful divorce.

Nikki lost her battle with cancer in 2006, about six years after marrying Shadrach. She had been diagnosed with melanoma in her teens and had not had any issues until the cancer resurfaced in about 2004. She first noticed a lump under her arm, and cancer eventually spread to her liver. By the time she died, cancer had spread throughout her body.

Shadrach explains that when she was diagnosed, he was scared and, of course, didn't want to lose her. She spent two years being treated with chemotherapy and experimental drugs. He says she had good days and bad days, and on the good days, they would make the most of it. Nikki didn't like being stuck inside the house, so they would leave when they could. Shadrach says that they had a good life together, and he is happy they shared many good times. Although I wasn't around to see the fight, I know she fought with grace and dignity.

She also struggled with the unfairness of it all. She wanted, and I think some days expected, to be able to use her story of cancer as a redemption story of God. I believe she had days she thought she would be healed. She and Shadrach made plans for the future.

But healing wasn't the story that God wrote for her. After spending the weekend away with some close friends and her mother, Nikki passed away in her childhood home on an early morning in May. She was surrounded by those who loved her. Nikki believed God would use her story of cancer to share his love, and I am sure he does.

If you ask the people who knew them, they will describe Shadrach and Nikki as perfect for each other. They complemented each other's strengths well and were good at building each other up. They enjoyed four wonderful years together, though the last two were marred with cancer treatments.

I know Shadrach and Nikki wanted children, but right when they decided to begin trying to conceive, Nikki's cancer returned. They were never able to achieve that dream together.

SHADRACH'S ABBY STORY

In 2006, a few months after Nikki passed and a few years after my divorce, I ran into Shadrach in a restaurant parking lot. I was just leaving as he was arriving, and I noticed him getting out of his car. At that point, he hadn't noticed me. I hesitated as I backed out of my parking spot, wondering if I should say something. After all, it had been a few years since we had talked, and he was walking into the restaurant with a group of people I didn't know. I didn't want to intrude. I wondered for a moment if he would even remember me. Totally out of my comfort zone (I am an introvert), I called out to him.

He and I began a conversation, and I learned that Nikki had passed away. Sometime later, the conversation continued when he called me. We started meeting up for lunches and, after a few months, started dating. We had some challenges. Navigating a dating life with a widower and a divorcee can be tricky at times. We both lived with the shadows of our histories.

But on a Tuesday afternoon, after a year of dating, we were married. The wedding took place on a beautiful spring day by a small lake with a few family and friends. It was amazing.

I often tell people that Shadrach and I were brought together because God clearly orchestrated it. This was our "God story."

Shadrach says he was "pleasantly surprised" when he learned I was pregnant. I think in Shadrach speak, this means he was really excited. He is even-keeled, low-key, and doesn't wear his emotions on his sleeve. When we decided to marry, he didn't know if we would have children. I believe this was in response to Nikki's death. As he watched his wife die, he came to think that making plans for the future only brought disappointment. If he had allowed himself to dream of children, he would have again been disappointed.

When we told Shadrach's family that I was pregnant, his dad said to me, "I am happy; I know Shadrach wants children." At that moment, I felt as if God was granting us both healing. Shadrach would find healing from losing Nikki, and I could have the family I had always dreamed of. We would have our happy ending.

Shadrach says he remained cautiously optimistic throughout my pregnancy until that final Saturday. He and I had finished the nursery, and he finally came to believe that this was "really happening."

The birth of our daughter became even more real to him the next day when I told him I was having contractions. On the way to the hospital, he remembers I told him that it was probably "nothing" and that the hospital would send me home. (I remember him driving too slowly.) He was sure we would be having a baby that day. He was thrilled to meet our baby girl.

When we arrived at the hospital, Shadrach was asked to wait in the hallway as they took me back to be examined. He suspected something was wrong because he was waiting a long time in a hallway with nowhere to sit. Another couple had come in while Shadrach was waiting, and that gentleman had been brought back before my husband. Then a nurse came out and said something vague, although he can't remember her words. This was when he became certain something was not right.

After he was brought back to join me, we heard there was

no heartbeat, and I was wheeled away to a room. On the way, a nurse told him, "You need to find a way to be there for her." He decided then and there that he had to take care of me so that I didn't succumb to depression. He was afraid I would never be okay again, that I would take to my bed and never leave. He was scared I would sink into a depression that would take me away from him, and he didn't want that to happen.

He was in the room during my surgery. He tells me that two doctors were in the operating room and a nurse whose job it was to count. He just remembers her counting. He was sitting by my head, holding my hand, and listening to the nurse count. He also responded to the nonsensical words I spoke under anesthesia.

While I was in recovery back in the room, he made phone calls and texted friends. He can't tell me which phone call was the most painful. I imagine him calling his dad first, though I'm not sure that's true. Shadrach finds a lot of comfort from his dad.

As I have mentioned before, I don't remember returning to the room, and I don't recall where Shadrach was or when I saw him next. I know he was sitting with me when I held Abby. In my mind, I have a clear image of a picture he took of our baby girl, and I have no idea when he did that. The day is a jumbled memory.

During that first day, Shadrach needed to go home to take care of our dogs. During his time at home, he yelled, not at anyone in particular, but at the world. He had no words, just sound. Hearing this, I was struck by the amount of pain he must have been in, losing his daughter, worried about his wife. My husband was triggered in that moment. He experienced feelings of what had just occurred while reexperiencing some loss from Nikki. He had already experienced, in his marriage to Nikki, many hospital visits, doctor's appointments, and treatments that weren't successful. He had been excited to bring home his daughter during this hospital visit. But it again ended in death. The story that he carries is that hospital visits end in death. My poor husband was in so much pain. He must have felt so much fear, and I didn't know. I regret that I was unable to be there for him emotionally.

He came back to the hospital, prepared to stay the night. He slept next to me on an uncomfortable pull-out chair. He endured a sleepless night, from both sadness and the nurses coming in and out. He didn't complain at all. He spent the next two nights on the pull-out chair.

During our hospital stay, I created more worry for Shadrach by announcing that I wouldn't be returning to work. I declared it: "How can I go back and sit with all those people?" This announcement came the day after Abby died, and Shadrach, in his quiet manner, took this information in and began working on a plan. He felt pressure to take care of us while I figured out where my career would take me.

Shadrach was concerned about me being by myself. He didn't want me alone with my thoughts. He wanted to make sure I was always okay, and if he couldn't be there with me, he worked hard to make sure someone else could. I didn't feel the need to have someone with me all the time, but I didn't want to fight him on it. If he needed that peace, I could give that to him.

Shadrach says that one of his fears was that this experience would break us as a couple. He needed me to know that he didn't blame me, that he loved me, and that I was important. He needed us to be okay. In my mind, even then, I never doubted that he and I would weather this storm. I felt his love in the ways he cared for me during that time, and I hope he never doubted my love for him.

Shadrach can't name a specific moment that he knew we would be okay. He felt more confident as time passed and steps were taken to return to life. We worked hard to lean on each other in the early days of grief.

I am grateful he was such a rock during that time. I am thankful he didn't blame me, even when, in the early days, I blamed myself. He and I never blamed each other as some couples do. I love that he made it a priority to show me that I was important.

During the hospital stay, without me being aware, Shadrach took care of Abby's arrangements. The day after Abby was delivered, Shadrach met with people at the mortuary. He says, "Those people have a special heart for the whole thing. They made something awful less awful." He left to go to the mortuary a few times while I was in the hospital and took care of all the arrangements. I remember him telling me that he picked out a teddy bear to hold Abby's ashes. My husband did that for our baby girl, which is one of the most loving things he could do. That makes my heart swell. That bear is a small representation of our daughter and a reminder of what a great dad Shadrach would have been.

I know of another baby-loss dad who fought to have his twins baptized before they left the hospital. It was hospital policy not to baptize children who had died, but his wife needed that for her own comfort, to protect her children. He found a way to make it happen. Many baby-loss parents are put into a position of needing to advocate for themselves and their child while in the hospital. This includes pastoral care and whether they want their child baptized. Hospitals don't often offer the opportunity for baptism or last rites, and if it is important to the parents, they may be put in the position where they have to ask. Hospitals have social workers who are there to offer support and guidance, but sometimes we need to advocate for ourselves. If it feels important to you, then feel the freedom to ask for it.

It is unfair, but Shadrach took the brunt of everything in those days. I was self-focused, and he carried the load for us both.

He was relieved when I was discharged, glad we could come home. He felt awful that I was in the maternity ward without our baby. He was "frustrated and disappointed" (Shadrach's terms for "angry") that the doctors couldn't tell us what had happened. He wanted answers as to what happened to our girl, and they couldn't tell us. After all the blood work and the autopsy, there were no answers.

Shadrach didn't return to work right away. At the time, he was working under a contract for a company near our home, which was a blessing. He had a good relationship with them, and they were gracious to allow him what he needed. I remember him being home much of August. That time is blurry, but I know he didn't require what I couldn't give, and I didn't ask for much from him. We spent a lot of time sitting quietly. We dug ourselves out of the hole together.

About a month after Abby died, we took a road trip. During that time, we scattered Abby's ashes and planted a rose bush in her honor. This must have been a reminder for

Shadrach of Nikki because a few years prior, he had sprinkled her ashes in the same river. We visit this place often, and we find peace there. During that trip, Shadrach and I spent time walking along beaches, and I experienced new places. I know Shadrach hoped I would feel happy when we returned home, and I wish I could have given that to him. Although I wasn't in the darkest pit of grief, I still longed for my daughter, continuing my healing journey.

A Second Pregnancy

A few months later, in November, we discovered that I was pregnant again. If you remember, Shadrach was terrified. We spent the next few weeks discussing how we would manage this pregnancy and what the next few months would look like. While I was in the hospital, some friends had come and put all the baby things in the nursery and closed the door. I hadn't even opened the door to Abby's room since we got home.

Shadrach was with me at that first doctor's appointment when we learned that the pregnancy wasn't viable.

We spent the holidays with family, and when we returned home, I went in for a D&C. This was the second time within months that Shadrach was put in the position of watching his wife go through surgery without bringing a child home. He says this experience brought up the feelings of being in the hospital, delivering Abby. What he didn't say, but I imagine is true, is that he was also reliving moments with Nikki in her cancer treatment. He hadn't had a lot of experience with positive outcomes of hospital treatments.

This was our last pregnancy. We attempted to get pregnant

through IVF and infertility treatments, but they were unsuccessful. After the IVF failed, we attempted adoption, which was also unsuccessful. We have come to accept that the story God has written for us doesn't include living children of our own. It is not the story we would have written, but it is our story.

In a conversation about Abby and this time in our lives, I asked Shadrach when he knew I was going to be okay. He said he felt confident in my ability to be okay about a year later. He knew I wasn't going to take to bed and never leave. He has gotten used to my rhythm. He knows that around August, I become sad. (We both do.) About three years after Abby died, around August, I was having an especially grief-filled time. This was about the same time that I gave up on being a mom to a living child. That year we decided it was time to donate most of Abby's things. We had kept her nursery intact since the hospital, and this was the first time since she had died that we went through all her things. We spent a day in her room, deciding which items to donate and which to get rid of.

We kept a few keepsake items. Some I didn't feel I could get rid of; others were special because of who gave them to us. That day was full of sorrow for us, probably one of the hardest since she had died.

That year Shadrach again became concerned that I would not be okay. He explained to me that he needed me to find my way out of the pit of sadness. Shadrach needed to know I would be okay. He needed us to continue living the story that God wrote for us. Just to clarify, he didn't ask me to let go of my grief or to be incongruent with my feelings. He asked me to hold firm to us and our life that we were carving out.

I have stopped seeking answers as to why Abby died, and

I think I have found new ways to use my story to help others. I like to think Abby would be proud of how our story has helped others in their healing.

I would be lying if I said I never had sad days of missing my girl. Some days it is harder to hold the grief with the love, and I find that some days tears come that I wasn't expecting. Unlike in the beginning of my journey, I no longer apologize for them. In the days that are harder, I allow myself extra grace, and I listen more closely to my body to hear what I might need. I am not always great at it. Some days I need to take off my shoes and walk through the grass to ground myself. On those days, I imagine my girl in her red Vans, walking beside me. And I am reminded that God is walking with us.

Questions for Reflection

Is there anything you wish others knew about your story?

If you have experienced child loss, what is your spouse's story? How is it similar or dissimilar to your own?

NOTES

Chapter 2: Miscarriage

1. "Miscarriage," Mayo Clinic, accessed December 16, 2020, https://www.mayoclinic.org/diseases-conditions/pregnancy-loss-miscarriage/symptoms-causes/syc-20354298.
2. "What Is Stillbirth?," Centers for Disease Control and Prevention, November 16, 2020, https://www.cdc.gov/ncbddd/stillbirth/facts.html.
3. "Signs of Miscarriage," American Pregnancy Association, April 26, 2020, https://americanpregnancy.org/healthy-pregnancy/pregnancy-complications/signs-of-miscarriage-916/.

Chapter 3: Now What?

1. "Miscarriage," March of Dimes, November 2017, https://www.marchofdimes.org/complications/miscarriage.aspx.
2. Violet Oaklander, *Windows to Our Children: A Gestalt Therapy Approach to Children and Adolescents* (Gouldsboro, ME: The Gestalt Journal Press, 1978), 11.

Chapter 4: Am I Crazy?

1. Bessel van der Kolk, *The Body Keeps the Score: Brain, Mind,*

and Body in the Healing of Trauma (New York: Penguin, 2015), 21.

2. Bessel van der Kolk, *How to Work with the Traumatized Brain*, National Institute for the Clinical Application of Behavioral Medicine.

3. Van der Kolk, *The Body Keeps the Score*, 21.

4. Van der Kolk, *The Body Keeps the Score*, 275.

5. Van der Kolk, *The Body Keeps the Score*, 210.

Chapter 6: The Gift of Being There

1. "What Are Possible Causes of Stillbirth?," National Institute of Child Health and Human Development, December 1, 2016, https://www.nichd.nih.gov/health/topics/stillbirth/topicinfo/causes.

Chapter 7: I Don't Want to Pray

1. Levi Lusko, *Through the Eyes of a Lion: Facing Impossible Pain, Finding Incredible Power* (Nashville: Thomas Nelson, 2015), 37.

2. Steven Curtis Chapman, *Between Heaven and the Real World: My Story* (Grand Rapids: Revell, 2017), 336.

3. Lusko, *Through the Eyes of a Lion*, 90.

Chapter 8: Am I Stuck?

1. Ronald Reagan, Proclamation 5890–Pregnancy and Infant Loss Awareness Month, 1988, www.reaganlibrary.gov/archives/speech/proclamation-5890-pregnancy-and-infant-loss-awareness-month-1988.